D1746302

THE MASTER ARCHITECT SERIES
MURPHY/JAHN
Selected and Current Works

Helmut Jahn · Oct. 02.

THE MASTER ARCHITECT SERIES
MURPHY/JAHN
Selected and Current Works

First published in Australia in 1995 by
The Images Publishing Group Pty Ltd
ACN 059 734 431
6 Bastow Place, Mulgrave, Victoria, 3170
Telephone (61 3) 561 5544 Facsimile (61 3) 561 4860

Copyright © The Images Publishing Group Pty Ltd 1995

All rights reserved. Apart from any fair dealing
for the purposes of private study, research,
criticism or review as permitted under the Copyright Act,
no part of this publication may be reproduced,
stored in a retrieval system or transmitted in
any form by any means, electronic, mechanical,
photocopying, recording or otherwise, without the
written permission of the publisher.

National Library of Australia Cataloguing-in-Publication Data

Jahn, Helmut, 1940-
    Murphy/Jahn: selected and current works.

    Bibliography.
    Includes index.
    ISBN 1 875498 19 2.
    Master Architect Series ISSN 1320 7253

    1. Murphy/Jahn (Firm). 2. Architecture, American.
    3. Architecture, Modern—20th century—United States.
    4. Architects—United States. I. Title. (Series: Master
    architect series).

    720.92

Edited by Stephen Dobney
Designed by The Graphic Image Studio Pty Ltd,
Mulgrave, Australia
Printed by Southbank Book,
Fishermans Bend, Australia

Contents

7 Introduction
Designing for the Urban Edge
By Ross Miller

Selected and Current Works

13   Mat Buildings

47   Tower Buildings

131 Urban Block Buildings

173 Transportation Buildings

Firm Profile

222 Offices of Murphy/Jahn, Architects

223 Cupola

224 Biography

225 Associates & Collaborators

228 Chronological List of Buildings & Projects

243 Awards & Exhibitions

253 Bibliography

261 Acknowledgments

262 Index

Introduction

Designing for the Urban Edge
By Ross Miller

Helmut Jahn's architecture first received wide attention in 1970 when he helped solve the challenging technical problem of building a new McCormick Place[1] on the foundations of the old. Assisting Gene Summers at the Chicago firm that now bears his name (Murphy/Jahn), Jahn demonstrated a rare quality that still marks his work today: the ability to move almost seamlessly from problem-solving—the technical side of architecture—to design.

A computer facility[2] has been added to the firm's two existing drafting rooms;[3/4] there is more model making and a greater reliance on written documentation because Jahn is often out of the office presenting new work or supervising ongoing projects; however, Murphy/Jahn still functions more as an atelier than a corporate architectural office. Architectural solutions are generated from the specific demands of the project and never imposed. Helmut Jahn is personally involved with every stage of the work in the office.

Since 1987, when the United Airlines Terminal[5/6] was completed at Chicago's O'Hare International Airport, Jahn has been closely associated with airport design. And airports are a useful point of departure for understanding Jahn's recent work. In analyzing the airport's evolving function in an increasingly decentralized global economy, Jahn has developed certain architectural forms that are now being elaborated upon at Munich and Cologne. Helmut Jahn recognizes that airports, in addition to their role of moving people and freight, have become self-sufficient economic and cultural nodes—micro-cities that are no longer dependent satellites of the old downtowns.

Introduction Continued

At Cologne/Bonn and Munich Airport Center⁷, Jahn's architecture recreates a nearly complete urban ambience of streets, loggias, and building facades within a sophisticated climate-controlled environment. The contemporary airport combines the mall (now a universal urban and suburban phenomenon) with the traditional transportation hub⁸.

For example, at Munich, along with the nearby Hotel Kempinski⁹, Jahn has turned his attention to refining the overall urban planning of this new "airport city". (See also the King Abdulaziz International and Bangkok International schemes.) Hotel Kempinski in the so-called "Neutral Zone" is the first non-flight-related building in the Munich master plan. The hotel creates a powerful spatial link between new and old. Both Kempinski and the Airport Center have large central rooms that break down normal divisions between interior and exterior space. A formal, French-style garden¹⁰ further eases the transition from high-technology geometry to nature. In most of Jahn's current work, landscape merges into architecture to create a completely specific environment. The airport is never opposed to the natural world but strives to complement it.

At Cologne/Bonn¹¹ the back-and-forth process of arrival is open and unimpeded with 40 "flow-thru" counters, and a succession of departure halls, concourses, and airplane gates. So Jahn's architecture, as well as developing a new city, also continues to streamline the airport's circulation and modernize its transportation function. The work is neither avant-garde nor conceptual, but highly refined in form and function.

Notable, too, is the architect's close attention to buildings that find themselves between main destinations, neither in town nor at the airport, but at the edge. The Hyatt Regency Roissy¹², located outside of Paris off the A1 Expressway, creates its own scale, using some of the tricks of introversion honed in the more complex airport schemes. The large garden atrium that separates the two five-story hotel blocks preserves some of the intimacy of the

Parisian courtyard hotel at an enlarged scale. This self-referential urbanism is applied to the Pallas Office Building[13] in Stuttgart and the Munich Order Center[14]. The Munich building does not attempt to overtly challenge the anonymity of its site in an industrial park outside the city, but rather creates its own semblance of a streetscape within the entrance courts of the linked units. The "guts" of the business all takes place above the "street", on the second and third floors. Visual variety is created through the exposed structural system of thick cables and tension plates.

Jahn consistently challenges the limits of a type while providing the best working example he can. As important as this "edge" work has been, Jahn's greatest contribution in this period has been in his urban commissions, particularly in Berlin. Kurfuerstendamm 70[15], his first building in Berlin, was appropriately on the only street of any real character left in the western half of the city after the war. All the great architecture—museums, opera houses, civic buildings—were marooned in the East. The Ku-Damm was a leftover street, notable for its nightlife and its deviation from the strict right-angled Berlin grid. Jahn modestly thinks of this important commission less as an original building than as "urban repair."

At a radically reduced scale, Ku-Damm 70 required the same rare mixture of talents as McCormick Place. In a misguided attempt in the 1950s to improve traffic and pedestrian flow, city planners had sheared three meters off the facade of the original building. After a competition, Jahn was retained to complete the restoration. By securing a variance to cantilever five meters over the sidewalk and exceed the city's 22-meter height limit, the architect found a way to build his first Berlin tower. Modest in scale—reminiscent in detailing of Frank Lloyd Wright's Price Tower and also of Mendelsohnian forms—this was the first architecture of the city's current period of rebuilding to find a useful modern idiom. The completed structure, fitted with a mast and crown, is a challenge to future builders to shape an architecture appropriate to Berlin's violent past and ongoing process of rebirth. Although

Introduction 9

Introduction Continued

personally apolitical, Jahn has inevitably become involved through his Berlin work. This involvement with politics and history has been good for his architecture.

Jahn's commercial buildings have sometimes lacked sufficient refinement of detail when there was not enough critical resistance or technical difficulty to temper the project. The paradox of Berlin is that the new center is the old edge. Jahn has been able to import many of the strategies of micro-urbanism perfected in the outlands of Munich and Paris to the former and future capital of Germany. At Stralauer Platz 35[16], he has managed to recall the concrete wall that bisected the site for 30 years and transform it into an ordering element of the project. He has effectively turned a wall into a sieve, making the mixed-use collection of commercial buildings (including a restored landmark) a catalog of classic urban elements—passage, loggia, gate, winter garden, terrace, park, and promenade—that re-introduce the city to the River Spree. At the Victoria-Berlin[17] renovation, Jahn applies the same sort of self-contained, refined urbanism—learned in the airport schemes and in process at Stralauer—to the Ku-Damm. Victoria is an elaborate repair that marries an exuberant expression of steel and glass to a dour existing building. Jahn's project suggests the spirit of Mendelsohn's lost Columbus Haus, completed before the war and purged, for decades, from civic memory.

In the 1960s the city of Berlin first tried to reach back to the diverse culture that had formed its architectural identity. Buildings by Schinkel and Mendelsohn, among others, had been blasted away. Those that remained were in ruin or horribly neglected under Soviet stewardship. The Kulturforum, off the already leveled Potsdamer Platz (the old center and Cold War edge), was conceived as an architectural challenge to the politicizing of culture in the East. Hans Scharoun's Philharmonie and Mies van der Rohe's National Gallery of Art were two radically different interpretations of architecture. One was expressionist and introverted, the other universal and polemical in its purity. Yet, taken together they reaffirmed the city's faith in itself and the value of imagination over ideology.

Helmut Jahn's 2.2 million square-foot Sony Center[18], within view of Scharoun's masterpiece, takes a good deal of inspiration from it. A huge, floating tent roof covers a "great space"—large enough to be outside but contained[19]. With theaters, businesses, electronic displays on the ground floor, and residences and offices above, the Sony Center is a reclaimed Potsdamer Platz for the new age of entertainment. The building is scheduled to open at 11:00p.m. on December 31, 1999. Jahn is serious about tailoring an architecture to the stimulating contemporary confusion of private and public space[20]. Sony Center is a kulturforum for the millennium in which the serious business of entertainment is portrayed as the real challenge to the high art of classical music and painting.

A portrait of Jahn's recent work would not be complete without an understanding of another side of his work. Along with the facility and exuberance of much of the Berlin work there are the towers, from the Fountain Square West project[21] in Cincinnati, to Singapore[22/23] and Kuala Lumpur. But it is with the 21 Century Tower[24] in Shanghai that one can get the best sense of where Helmut Jahn is heading. The Shanghai skyscraper has all the facility of his earlier work but with a commanding simplicity. Normally necessary elements, such as a wrapping glass wall, are scrupulously removed, until the structure is the building: its skeleton and ornament. Landscape elements—the impression of a tropical garden overtaking a lattice—enrich the architecture; they are not simply added for effect. As in the best of the latest work, disciplined simplicity makes Helmut Jahn's work brilliantly complex.

Ross Miller's most recent book is *American Apocalypse: The Great Fire and the Myth of Chicago*. In Fall 1995 Alfred A. Knopf will publish *City Games*, a comprehensive study of the American city after urban renewal. His writing has appeared in the *Wall Street Journal, Progressive Architecture* and the *Los Angeles Times*, among other national publications.

Introduction 11

Selected and Current Works

Mat Buildings

14	Munich Order Center
20	Celebration Center
22	Navy Pier
23	San Diego Convention Center
24	Wisconsin Residence
28	ANL/DOE Program Support Facility
30	Area 2 Police Headquarters
32	De La Garza Career Center
34	Rust-Oleum Corporation Headquarters
36	Saint Mary's Athletic Facility
38	Michigan City Public Library
40	Auraria Library
42	Abu Dhabi Conference Center City
43	Minnesota Government & History Center
44	Kemper Arena

Munich Order Center

Design/Completion 1989/1993
Munich, Germany
Archimedes Gewerbe und Buero Centrum GmbH & Co.
1,500,000 square feet
Composite steel and concrete frame, cable-stayed steel and glass roof
Glass and aluminum curtain wall

The Munich Order Center (MOC) evolved from a program combining large public exhibit halls for industry shows with small private showrooms (order offices). These two uses have opposite architectural requirements, yet the MOC binds both together with an efficient regular structure and generous public spaces.

The backbone of the building is the service wall in which the mechanical systems, elevators and exit stairs are concentrated. Extruded from the service wall are cable-stayed roofs spanning 78 feet, split at their peaks by skylights. The longest roofs define "solid fingers" which house the order offices on the building's upper two floors and extend the full length of the site. The intervening "open fingers" enclose the building's major spaces, namely the entrance courts, ground-level foyer, first-floor linear atria, and the tree-lined promenade. A bridge spans the promenade, linking the north and south tracts of the building mass.

1   Site plan
2   Detail sketch
3   Front facade
4   Restaurant pavilion
5   Entry court
6–7 Sun shades

3

4
5

6
7

Munich Order Center 15

8   Ground-floor plan/sections
9   Louvered service wall
10 Promenade with bridge linking north and south buildings
11 Fritted pattern wall detail

11

12 a–d Structural/wall details
13 Mast/outrigger/cable tie-down
14 Bridge king post
15 Entrance from second floor with bridge
16 Exhibitors' display area
17 Exhibitors' common area with skylights
18 Seating areas with patterned glass wall
19 Exhibit hall entrance
20 Private office corridor

15

16

17

18

19

20

Munich Order Center 19

Celebration Center

Design 1991
Orlando, Florida
Disney Development Co.
1,500,000 square feet
Steel frame
Glass infill, fabric and glass roof

Celebration Center is an attempt to rethink the regional mall on functional, technical, aesthetic and experiential levels; to transfer the urban experience of shopping to the suburban realm. Regional shopping centers are generally diagrams of circulation and space management. In contrast, urban shopping is a rich and varied mixture of commerce, culture, recreation and ceremony.

The overall image is of a city surrounded by "green walls" of vines growing on constructed frames, with giant "gates" giving appropriate scale to the various shopping precincts. Beyond the "gates" are the parking garages or surface parking lots. From here, visitors proceed through side streets and town squares to the curved main streets and the open spaces.

The typologies of main street, side street, arcade, town square, ceremonial park, festival park, science park and nature park have been taken from the traditional city and transformed and abstracted. The resulting system provides a fixed circulation system with spaces and uses that are flexible and adaptable.

1 Concept sketch
2 Town squares
3 Enclosing "green wall" with frame and "gates"
4 Main street, arcade, town squares, retail and parking
5 Arcade
6 Nature park
7 "Green wall"
8 Festival park

Celebration Center

Navy Pier

Design 1991
Chicago, Illinois
Metropolitan Pier and Exhibition Authority
500,000 square feet
Steel frame
Glass infill, fabric and glass roof

Navy Pier is not a single building, but a flexible arrangement of structures that allow a variety of different activities. Steel arcades are the connecting elements between the east and west wings. These contain the mechanical and electrical systems. Simple, arched steel girders can be spanned between the two buildings whenever space or a roofed area becomes necessary. The open spaces, bound by arcades, are left uncovered. This system allows for many closed, covered and open spaces, and guarantees the important continuity of the pier's profile.

From the outside, Navy Pier is a clear, linear object. Inside, it is a series of buildings, spaces and experiences: a linear city, which grows out into Lake Michigan. The pier landscape expands the public space of the lake-shore-park with a series of strong, visually exciting and useful public spaces.

1 Winter garden
2 Restaurants
3 Ferris wheel and observation platform within open linear series of spaces with areas of arched steel girders

San Diego Convention Center

Design 1984
San Diego, California
San Diego Convention Bureau
Joint Venture Architects: Martinez/Wong Associates Inc.
690,000 square feet
Steel frame with long-span folded trusses
Glass curtain wall and metal panels

The architect's foremost intention was to create a truly public building, devoid of the hermetically sealed character of most convention centers, which turn their back towards the city.

The entry functions and vertical movement corridors face the city and are revealed through glass walls. Public terraces face the water and are accessible by a ramp system from the boardwalk. Connecting the internal access with the public access is the Great Hall which serves as the entry to all meeting functions.

The architectural themes in this building are nautical images which can be identified with San Diego—lighthouses, masts, guy-wires, decks, bridges and cranes.

The footprint of the building is generated by the confines of the site. The forms of the building's distinct parts are enhanced by surface treatment and ornament, generated by structural and constructional necessities. Thus the building recalls much of the glass and steel architecture of the great exhibition buildings of the past.

1 Lighthouses are a strong nautical image identified with San Diego
2 The Great Hall incorporates masts, bridges and cranes

Wisconsin Residence

Design/Completion 1980/1982
Eagle River, Wisconsin
2,500 square feet
Wood frame
Insulated glass and wood panels

The house, for a family of three, is planned as a vacation home, with the understanding that it may become a year-round residence at a later date. The building provides indoor living space and outdoor terraces on three levels. Also planned are an outdoor screened pavilion located near the water and a small marina. The site comprises 3.5 acres of lakefront property in northern Wisconsin. The house is located in the center of a wooded slope, affording views of the lake and opposite shore.

With its entry bridge, stair tower and lake pavilion, the house establishes a strong geometric presence on this lakeshore site. The structural and symbolic gridded shapes present themselves in sharp focus through the surrounding cover. Further reinforcing the (ideal object) quality of these forms is their sequential composition, designed to be a descending procession from hilltop to shore. The house itself is elevated in the center of this procession by a classically inspired cornice.

1–2 Helmut Jahn sketches
3 Night lighting of cube form
4 Lake elevation
5 Terrace entry upper level

Wisconsin Residence   25

6

7
8

6 Side elevation with entrance bridge
7 Overall view with stair to lakefront
8 Terrace
9 Living area
10 Vertical stair core
11 Kitchen/eating areas

9

10

11

Wisconsin Residence 27

ANL/DOE Program Support Facility

Design/Completion 1978/1981
Argonne, Illinois
US Department of Energy
215,000 square feet
Steel frame
Clear anodized aluminum panels and sun shades, green painted mullions, silver painted structure and extensive skylighting

The program called for office and support space for the Chicago Branch of the Department of Energy and the Argonne National Laboratories. The brief envisages the building as a pilot demonstration project for passive solar energy use, the use of solar collectors, and energy-conscious design. The design disrupts the natural wooded setting of the site as little as possible. The round shape was generated in response to the road network, the non-directional character of the site, and (on a symbolic level) by the association it evokes with the sun as an energy source. A segment of the circle is removed to provide south orientation for the location of the future solar collectors. These collectors will step back to provide exterior shading for the glazed area. The amount of western exposure is minimized to reduce peak air-conditioning loads.

The round shape is completed by a retention pond which increases reflectivity for the solar collectors and daylight entering the building.

1   Third-floor plan and site plan
2   South-facing facade, sun shading and entrance
3   Curved side wall
4   Entrance
5   Vestibule
6   Light shafts maximizing natural daylight

ANL/DOE Program Support Facility   29

Area 2 Police Headquarters

Design/Completion 1977/1982
Chicago, Illinois
135,000 square feet
Steel frame
Blue insulated metal panels with panels of clear and frosted insulating glass block

This government building serves a multitude of functions: area police center, district police center, police detention center, courts complex, sheriff's security complex, and vehicle maintenance facility.

The varied functions generate a range of configurations within a 660-foot long and 170-foot wide continuous building. The location of the building on the site creates zones for public and staff parking.

The public entry is through an open courtyard, which can also be used for community-related gatherings. This entry court ties into the circulation system which is clear and comprehensible, and provides the necessary separation of public and private activities.

Wall materials were chosen to provide as much natural light as possible, creating an openness not often found in this building type. All walls on the building's long sides are of glass block with bands of clear insulating glass where uses demand outside orientation. The court is completely glazed, and the end walls are of insulated metal panels.

1 Section with central court and flying structure
2 Street facade and public access
3 Blue metal panel with infill of clear and frosted glass block
4 Internal stair
5 Lobby

4

5

Area 2 Police Headquarters 31

De La Garza Career Center

Design/Completion 1976/1980
East Chicago, Indiana
City of East Chicago
106,000 square feet
Steel frame
Press-formed steel sash, insulated panels and gasket glass

A vocational high school building containing shops, classrooms and support space, the center is sited to separate public access from services and parking. Shops are located in an 80-foot-wide high-bay area; classrooms and support spaces are in an 80-foot-wide, two-story tract with 40-foot bays.

This arrangement allows for the clear linear organization of functions, the efficient use of space, and the consolidation of major program elements. The organization is expressed at the short ends where the structure is left exposed, revealing the building section and also providing for future expansion in that direction.

Standard systems are used for speed of construction, quality control and cost benefits. The structure is of truss, girders and joists on pipe columns; the exterior wall is of press-formed steel sash and insulated panels and gasketed glass; interior walls are masonry.

1 Sketch: site plan
2 Sketch: circulation, classroom and shop area
3 End wall elevation with mechanical unit
4 Green structure/yellow enclosure
5 Entrance
6 Shop entrance
7 Two-story shop area with expressed building systems

3

4

5

6

7

De La Garza Career Center   33

Rust-Oleum Corporation Headquarters

Design/Completion 1976/1978
112,000 square feet (includes half of parking area below building)
Vernon Hills, Illinois
Rust-Oleum Corporation
90,000 square feet
Exposed steel frame with metal deck
Alternate layers of glass and white enameled metal panels

The building explores ideas of circulation and movement, the use of natural light, and the creation of a pleasant, humane working environment.

In order to preserve the available site area for landscaping, the structure is raised above the covered parking area that provides space for 112 cars. Employees enter from the parking level through secured lobbies, while visitors enter through level 1.

A central organizing spine is the three-dimensional circulation axis, and contains all building services. The skylight space creates openness and orientation and separates the office space into four flexible and modular areas which can be parceled according to changing requirements.

The exterior walls are completely glazed to strengthen the inside–outside relationship. Alternating horizontal bands of glass and aluminium reinforce the horizontal character of the building.

1 Site plan
2 Front elevation
3 Elevation sketch
4 Floor plan/circulation sketch
5 Circulation axis

3 EAST ELEVATION   TYP. SECTION

4 FLOOR 1

Rust-Oleum Corporation Headquarters   35

Saint Mary's Athletic Facility

Design/Completion 1976/1977
South Bend, Indiana
St Mary's College
42,000 square feet
Steel frame with long-span trusses
Translucent insulated fiberglass panels and a curved clerestory

The primary use of the structure is as an athletics facility; however, it can also function as an exhibit or assembly facility for graduations, concerts, or social events. It contains two flexible multi-purpose areas, two racquetball courts, lockers, faculty offices, student lounge, lobby, and common support and utility space. Bleacher seating accommodates 1,800 people for spectator sports.

The racquetball courts and support spaces, which are fixed in size and use, are located on two floors at one end of the building. Adjacent to this is the high-bay multi-purpose area for tennis, volleyball and basketball. Gymnastics, dance and fencing are accommodated in a low-bay area at the other end of the structure.

Two circulation trunks along the perimeter of the upper level connect all functional elements, and establish the order and organization for expansion.

1 Floor plan/sections
2 Concept sketches
3 Front elevation
4 Playing field with spectators area
5 Playing field with clerestory
6 Integrated mechanical system
7 Multi-purpose area/playing field
8 Entrance/circulation trunk/clerestory

Saint Mary's Athletic Facility 37

Michigan City Public Library

Design/Completion 1974/1977
Michigan City, Indiana
Public Library System
35,000 square feet
Exposed steel frame with steel joists
Translucent insulated fiberglass panels with north-oriented clerestory

The building serves as the main branch facility for the Michigan City Public Library system. It occupies a downtown site, creating a spatial closure to Franklin Mall, the main commercial spine.

The building contains areas for adult services, reference and information, children's services, audiovisual resources, technical services, administration, and a business office. Common areas include the lobby, circulation desk and a flexible meeting room complex.

The program is organized within a one-story "loft space". An interior court is located asymmetrically along the diagonal axis. All office and work areas are located along the perimeter enclosed by free-standing partitions. Only the permanent and movable walls of the meeting room complex extend to the structure and roof to provide acoustical privacy.

1. Plan
2. Entrance with clerestory
3. Perimeter circulation corridor
4. Translucent exterior wall
5. The interior landscaped courtyard

Michigan City Public Library 39

Auraria Library

Design/Completion 1974/1976
Denver, Colorado
Auraria Higher Education District
184,000 square feet
One-way, post-tensioned cast-in-place concrete; reinforced concrete
Aluminum skin of fixed glass, operating sash and insulated metal panels

The building serves as the central Learning Resources Center for a new college in Denver, and contains library, media production and media education facilities. The organization of the building into two levels above grade and a partial basement reflects its different functional elements: the media production center requires no natural light, while the reading and support space of the library require maximum exposure.

The two floors are developed as flexible "loft space". Two open courts placed asymmetrically within the plan subdivide each floor into various "use" areas, accommodate outdoor reading, and provide natural light and outside air. Three open stairways connect the two levels. Except for a set core on the two levels, all individual rooms are placed along the perimeter.

1 Entry/exit lobby
2 Public catalog
3 Reference
4 Inter-library loan
5 Reserve
6 Media education entrance
7 Periodicals
8 Vestibule
9 Shipping
10 Technical services
11 Outdoor reading
12 General
13 Mechanical
14 TV studio
15 Conference
16 Duplication
17 Typing
18 Circulation

1 Plan
2 Front elevation with sun shades
3 Glass wall with sun shades

Auraria Library 41

Abu Dhabi Conference Center City

Design 1976
United Arab Emirates
Steel truss operable room with concrete substructure
Punched metal panels, sun shades and laminated glass

This prize-winning concept developed by C.F. Murphy Associates in an international competition for a conference city in Abu Dhabi, United Arab Emirates, represents a unique approach to the problems of transportation, urban design, environmental impact, and energy conservation.

This city is to be located on a narrow peninsula in the Persian Gulf where the midday temperatures reach 120°F. The major facility on the site, the conference center, includes an assembly hall for delegation meetings, large exhibition spaces, restaurants, meeting rooms, and facilities for the world press. The plan also includes housing for delegates, visiting heads of State and other dignitaries and related support and service functions.

The main element in the organization of the city is the automated personal transit system which connects the major elements of the conference center, residences, service areas, and mode transfer points. The spatial concept is one of a complete climate-controlled environment between the circulation trunks.

1 Section/perspective
2 Delegate housing with conference court in background and movable sun-shading roof

42 Abu Dhabi Conference Center City

Minnesota Government & History Center

Design 1976
St Paul, Minnesota
State of Minnesota
Cast-in-place reinforced concrete
Laminated glass-covered winter garden

The building forms part of the existing Capitol complex, and houses the Minnesota Historical Society Museum as well as classroom space, public meeting rooms for legislative and state agency hearings, an auditorium, a public cafeteria and parking for 450 cars.

The building is completely below grade, allowing the landscaping to be the form-giving and directional element. This enhances and reinforces existing vistas and creates a more pedestrian-oriented precinct. A succession of spatial experiences leads to a large rectangular open space appropriate to the classical dignity and formality of the site.

The circulation system relates the public spaces in the building to a grand, glass-covered garden that extends most of the way between the State Office Building and the Historical Society Building. This space contains a garden restaurant and is open to all levels of the new building.

1 Site plan
2 Underground complex and glass-covered garden with Capitol building in the background

Kemper Arena

Design/Completion 1973/1974
Kansas City, Missouri
American Royal Arena Corporation
17,000 seats
Steel pipe trusses with secondary steel joists
Insulated metal panels

The brief called for a multi-purpose indoor arena seating 1,000 to 18,000 people to be used for hockey, basketball, and boxing; track events; musical and variety programs; horse and livestock shows; and conventions. The development occupies a former stockyards site in an industrial district undergoing redevelopment.

The building is a single-story structure with two major elements: the substructure (including the seating), and the superstructure and building enclosure. The substructure is of reinforced concrete. The seating in the upper tier is of L-shaped precast, prestressed concrete elements on cast-in-place bents. For the superstructure, the major subsystems of steel structure, steel decking and steel cladding panel system enabled the basic envelope to be completed in a short time.

The ground level of the structure is buried in an earth berm, which provides a walkway around the building at concourse level. The oval form of the concourse level transforms into a rectangle at the upper level through the addition of four mechanical rooms.

1 Lower and upper level seating plan/section
2 Interior arena seating
3 West elevation/section
4 West elevation
5 Rigid bent main exterior structure
6 Detail of tube elements

Kemper Arena 45

Selected and Current Works

Tower Buildings

48	Jakarta Communications Tower
49	Jakarta Tower Kuningan Centre
50	21 Century Tower
54	Endless Towers
55	Tokyu-Shibuya Tower
56	Hitachi Tower/Caltex House
66	Fort Canning Tower
67	IHZ Tower
68	120 North LaSalle
72	Messe Tower/Messe Hall
80	Fountain Square West
82	FAA O'Hare Control Tower
83	Kuala Lumpur City Center 1
84	Barnett Center
86	Yokohama Waterfront MM21
88	Tokyo Teleport Town
90	425 Lexington Avenue
92	750 Lexington Avenue
94	Cityspire
95	Project J (1, 2, 3)
96	Wilshire/Westwood
100	1111 Brickell Avenue
101	The North Loop Block 37
102	Oakbrook Terrace Tower
104	One Liberty Place
108	Northwestern Atrium Center
112	362 West Street
114	Park Avenue Tower
116	Metro West
118	South Ferry Plaza
119	Columbus Circle
120	Bank of Southwest Tower
122	11 Diagonal Street
124	Chicago Board of Trade Addition
126	One South Wacker
128	Xerox Centre

Jakarta Communications Tower

Design 1995
Jakarta, Indonesia
PT Kuningan Persada
1,500,000 square feet
Braced steel frame
Aluminum frame with infill glass and aluminum louvers

This telecommunications tower for television, radio, satellite, and microwave transmissions will become a major national symbol of Indonesia.

Two alternatives were studied: a tower only, and a tower with an office building at its base. An amenity building with retail, convention, entertainment, and parking facilities surrounds the tower and links it to its urban setting.

The plan configuration is a tripod. The structure is a triangulated perimeter tube. The low aspect ratio of the structure and the braced perimeter system minimize steel weight and deflections. A glass skin covers the main faces of the triangle. The observation and restaurant levels project out from the tower in pinwheel fashion, permitting views of Jakarta, the sea, and the tower itself. A holographic artwork symbolizing Indonesia's five principles of philosophy crowns the top of the tower.

1 Tower option
2 Tower/office option

Jakarta Tower Parcel 8 Kuningan Center

Design 1994
Jakarta, Indonesia
Pacific Metrorealty
1,448,000 square feet
Steel frame with seismic superframe and modular gravity frame
Glass in aluminum mullion system, steel trellis, precast panels, stone faced panels and stone grid systems

The design for Jakarta Tower combines the geometric simplicity of the square and circle with the beauty and dynamics of the spiral, representing progress and an ascendent future. It also represents a synergy of tropical garden and high-rise building.

The subtle spiral expressed in the curtain wall is articulated by set-back terraces with vine-covered trellis rising the full height of the building. A tinted soffit at the set-back areas insures a clear reading of the building motif from all angles.

The tower is located on a retail base which provides its urban context. A network of gallerias and arcades integrates the office, banking, and retail functions. The central retail atrium is defined by walkways of clear geometries which overlay a common structural grid. Canopies and sunscreens foster connections and linkages as well as insuring user comfort and flexibility of functions.

1 Concept sketches
2 Spiral curtain wall with set-back vine-covered terraces
3 Entrance axis

21 Century Tower

Design/Completion 1993/1997
Shanghai, China
Everbright International Trust and Investment Corp.
Associate Architect: East China Architectural Design Institute
862,400 square feet
Steel frame
Painted red panels, blue and green glass with black frit pattern and gray frames

21 Century Tower will occupy a unique site in the heart of the Lujiazui Finance and Trade Zone of the Pudong New Area, facing the Shanghai Bund.

The project consists of two components: the 49-story tower and the three-story podium building. Five nine-story skygardens form a third major element. These landscaped gardens are spaces to be used for informal meetings, meals or relaxation. Their structure is independent of the tower, and supports a glass facade which provides protection from the environment.

The structural principle employed for the tower is that of a braced tube. The structural system eliminates the column at the north-east corner which fronts the east–west axis, marking the ceremonial entrance and identifying the skygarden locations. The podium building, at the south-west corner of the site, is treated as a pavilion that is separated programmatically from the tower, but is tied to it by a system of canopies that provide covered passage.

1 Concept sketches
2 Skygarden
3 Five nine-story skygardens
4 The axis reinforces the master plan's ceremonial axis
5 A singular object expressing transparency, color and structure

21 Century Tower

6   Blue and green glass reinforces the structural pattern
7   Skygardens are glazed in clear glass with stucture in red
8   Ceremonial entrance and three-story podium detail
9   The structure is that of a braced tube

21 Century Tower

Endless Towers

Design 1995
Theoretical high-rise project
1,865,662 square feet
Mega-structure framing of steel box sections forming an external tube
Skin of reflective glass, patterned spandrel glass, high-performance clear glass at skygardens, solar glass at interior walls at skygardens

This project consists of two similar towers in which the container is juxtaposed with the contained. The bold simplicity of the forms is inspired by the artist Brancusi.

Tower 1 expresses the structural endless column system in a bold graphic pattern. Tower 2 extends the immateriality of the container beyond the building's top into a roof garden.

The alternating symmetry of the chamfered corners defines a trussed tube. The mega-structure utilizes this architectural form to obtain efficient vertical and lateral load-resisting systems.

The skygardens provide quality space, panoramic views, and a more pleasant working environment. They are also an important part of the towers' environmental control systems, providing a buffer zone betweeen the office space and the outdoor conditions.

1–2 Concept sketches
3 Interplay of building towers in the city context

54 Endless Towers

Tokyu-Shibuya Tower

Design 1992
Tokyo, Japan
Tokyu Corporation
Associate Architect: Kume Sekkei Co. Ltd/Media Five
1,022,571 square feet
Structural steel, glass curtain wall
Granite floor and plaza

The slightly skewed plan of the Tokyu-Shibuya Tower generates an elegant, distinctive and omni-directional shape. The building form is accentuated further through inflections on the facade, and the top is sloped to complete the sculptural composition.

The building comprises two main components: the hotel/office tower and the wedding hall/conference center. A glass-covered porte-cochere separates the two components. The first floor of the conference center contains the lobby and the wedding hall. A main ballroom is on the second floor. An enclosed bridge over the porte-cochere at the mezzanine level connects to the hotel tower.

The porte-cochere also serves as the entry to the hotel. Restaurants and shops are at the ground floor, and a tea lounge is on the mezzanine level. A landscaped garden serves as a backdrop to this space. Express elevators take hotel guests from the ground floor to the main hotel lobby and front desk at the eighteenth floor.

1 Site plan
2 Expression of hotel/office tower and conference center

Hitachi Tower/Caltex House

Design/Completion 1988/1993
Savu Properties Pte.
Associate Architect: Architects 61
Hitachi Tower: 375,000 square feet
Caltex House: 400,000 square feet
Tower: steel frame and reinforced concrete core
Arcade: exposed steel frame
Aluminum panels, glass infill, structure glazing and marble floors

Located at the historic Change Alley Arcade, Hitachi Tower and Caltex House have a significance that must work on two levels: continuing an evolving urban context and establishing an identity on the Singapore skyline. Change Alley has historically been an important venue for changing money and purchasing local handicrafts. This arcade now finds itself as part of Singapore's ever-growing financial district.

The design of the towers creates a gateway to an important pedestrian street linking the sea and Collyer Quay with Raffles Square, the financial district and the towers that comprise the new Singapore.

The elements of Hitachi Tower—shaft and podium—reinforce the urban condition along Collyer Quay. The 38-story tower is rendered as a one-story frame with a setback at the twenty-fourth floor. A metal bay is juxtaposed with the background frame in order to introduce a scale element and reinforce the orientation to the sea.

Continued

1 Hitachi Tower: concept sketch
2 Hitachi Tower: front/harbor elevation

The "free" geometry of the ground floor reinforces pedestrian movement in and around the site. Small shops line the arcade to foster movement to Raffles Square. A cool palate of white, grey and blue is utilized as a welcome relief to the tropical atmosphere of Singapore.

The organization of Caltex House is that of a four-story retail podium and arcade with an office tower of 29 stories rising above. The rounded end of the tower offers views of Raffles Square, while also generating the top of the tower and providing a four-story entry portico.

Four levels of retail extend the retail component of Hitachi Tower in a style that is sympathetic in detail and material. The 72-foot high arcade space is topped with a glass roof offering protection from the elements, but providing ample natural light. The enclosure of the tower is rendered in metal and glass, similar to Hitachi Tower.

3 Hitachi Tower: curtain wall detail
4 Hitachi Tower: harbor view from the south-east with metal panel service wall
5 Hitachi Tower: harbor view from the north-east

Hitachi Tower/Caltex House 59

6

7

8

6 Level 2 galleria toward Hitachi
7 Entrance Caltex/Subway
8 Caltex glass wall entrance
9 Hitachi Tower: elevator cab
10 Hitachi Tower: elevator lobby
11 Hitachi Tower lobby

Hitachi Tower/Caltex House

12 Retail galleria section
13 Retail passageway from Caltex House
14 Level 3 galleria toward Caltex House
15 Caltex House: concept sketch
16 Caltex House: skylobby

15

16

Hitachi Tower/Caltex House 63

GROUND-FLOOR PLAN

TYPICAL LOW-RISE PLAN

TYPICAL HIGH-RISE PLAN

PENTHOUSE PLAN

ROOF PLAN

0 16.5 33 66ft
0 5 10 20m

17

17 Tower plans
18 Caltex House from the north
19 Caltex House: brow project spandrel
20 Caltex House: glass/metal banding

Hitachi Tower/Caltex House 65

Fort Canning Tower

Design 1992
Singapore
Singapore Telecom
Associate Architect: Architects 61
Height: 950 feet
Steel frame with stainless steel cladding

The tower is designed to be adaptable to meeting changing social, political and technical needs. Formally the tower is a helix-wound perforated steel plate coupled to the mast with outriggers. The negative surface is comprised of a lattice steel structure, making the tower at once solid and transparent. The steel tower rests upon a granite plinth housing radio equipment and the visitors' lobby.

The tower is sited at the Terrace View Garden which serves as the forecourt. A rolling hedge garden completes the circular form, and the tower is sited asymmetrically within this composition.

The structure embodies the principle of tube within tube to provide a stiff, slender structural platform to satisfy the deflection limitations of the telecommunications systems. These systems are housed in discrete pods at the most efficient level in terms of structural considerations and distance from antennas.

1   The communications tower becomes a symbol for Singapore

IHZ Tower

Design 1992
Düsseldorf, Germany
Premier GmbH Bouygues
880,100 square feet
Steel with major and minor frame development
Glass and aluminum curtain wall, aluminum columns, granite, textured metal panels and aluminum grid structures

The site for IHZ Tower lies in an evolving master-planned development in Düsseldorf. The primary urban planning goal is not to conform to the existing context, but to lead and invigorate the realization of the future-oriented project.

The form of IHZ Tower derives from the functional need to provide clear, efficient, well-lit office space. Composed of two parallel office wings connected by a core and service areas, the tower features floor plates offering well-oriented office layouts, complete flexibility in leasing, and economy in construction. At lower levels the tower is connected to an auxiliary structure providing for single-floor tenants.

Terraces created at levels 14 and 26 provide feature areas for the restaurant, cafeteria, and club facilities, which are located to take advantage of the exterior space.

The auxiliary building contains a business center and other communal functions. A central lobby/atrium separates the two project components.

1   View from the north-east showing the interplay of structure and skin
2   Concept sketch

120 North LaSalle

Design/Completion 1988/1991
Chicago, Illinois
Ahmanson Commercial Development Corporation
576,900 square feet
Placed concrete, steel at vaults
Polished Rockville, honed Raphaela, and flamed Galizia granites; gray tinted glass and patterned fritted spandrel glass

The building's location on a narrow mid-block site in LaSalle Street, one of the city's most highly defined urban spaces, generated its particular forms and spaces.

The inherent asymmetry of the site led to a structure that is asymmetrical in plan and elevation. All fixed elements are contained in a compact side-core to provide adjacent unobstructed office space of maximum flexibility. A curved bay extends over LaSalle Street, responding to the limited corner condition at Court Place. The projecting bay affords excellent views down LaSalle Street and to the river, giving the space a unique character.

A coved loggia with a large mosaic mural brings the public realm into the site. A projecting trellis extends through Court Place and to the entrances at LaSalle and Wells Streets, enhancing the pedestrian experience of this well-traveled mid-block link to City Hall.

1–2 Concept sketches
3 Pedestrian view of curved loggia and projecting bay

3

120 North LaSalle   69

4

4 Gridded north wall, trellis, projecting glass bay and curved blades at top
5 Asymmetrical stone service core
6 Entrance lobby
7 Elevator lobby
8 Streetscape

Messe Tower/Messe Hall

Design/Completion 1985/1991 (Tower), 1985/1988 (Exhibition Hall)
Tower: TishmanSpeyer Properties of Germany, LP
Exhibition Hall: Messe Halle Messe Frankfurt GmbH
Tower: 971,000 square feet
Exhibition Hall: 820,680 square feet
Tower: Poured-in-place concrete
Panelized curtain wall with red granite, painted aluminum mullions, patterned and clear glass
Exhibition Hall: Poured-in-place concrete, steel trusses
Metal and glass panel wall systems

The client's brief called for a new exhibition hall with 215,000 square feet of exhibition space, an entry building, a rentable office building, and 900 parking spaces. The 1909 Festhalle built by Friedrich von Thiersch, and the post-war Kongresshalle are immediately adjacent. Together with these two buildings, the new Exhibition Hall (Halle 1) forms a border to the outdoor exhibition space, which is open to the avenue and park of the Friedrich-Ebert-Anlage.

The office building is freestanding and is placed like a campanile among the composition of low buildings. The tower is raised high above the ground to create a symbolic gate to the Messe.

The architectural themes—long span hall, arcade, pavilion, tower, campanile, and gate—are elaborated in the forms of the buildings and their subtle relationships. Pure geometric forms—the square, circle, cylinder, and pyramid—are interrelated, rotated, transformed and elaborated in the materials and detailing.

1 Tower sketches
2 Site plan
3 Messe fairground relative to the city of Frankfurt

4

5

6

74

4 Entrance gate
5 Cylindrical glass entrance with canopy
6 Lobby
7 Pyramid top with glass cylinder
8 Public plaza
9 Section/plans

Messe Tower/Messe Hall 75

10 City view with registration pavilion showing punched stone wall with glass cylinder
11 Exhibition Hall and registration pavilion
12 Aerial view of Exhibition Hall

11

12

Messe Tower/Messe Hall 77

13

14 15

13 Registration pavilion and public plaza
14 Exhibition Hall truss/column connection
15 Exhibition Hall elevation
16 Truss/column connection detail
17 Glass end wall
18 Registration/entry pavilion interior
19 Exhibition Hall interior
20 Exterior roof truss
21 Roof truss, mechanical, service corridor

Fountain Square West

Design 1991
Cincinnati, Ohio
The Galbreath Company
1,200,000 square feet
Steel frame with concrete core
Steel superstructure clad in stainless steel; curtain wall infill of insulating vision glass, fritted spandrel glass; fluoropon-coated aluminum

Fountain Square West is one of few remaining sites in downtown Cincinnati of great urban significance, occupying the length of Fifth Street with prominent frontages along Race and Vine Streets. This project imaginatively integrates all functions within a mixed-use complex. The high-rise tower contains 750,000 square feet of corporate office space and a 250-room hotel. Some 175,000 square feet of retail is provided on three levels within the base, with parking for 750 automobiles below.

The retail base concentrates its focus on Race Street, the traditional downtown retail street, while the office tower and hotel functions focus on Fountain Square itself. Fountain Square West would rise above the city, reshaping the downtown skyline, and becoming the focal point for Cincinnati.

1 Concept sketch of building alternatives
2 Concept sketch of skin detail
3 City context: street view
4 Projecting front bay

FAA O'Hare Control Tower

Design 1991
Chicago, Illinois
Chicago O'Hare International Airport/Department of Aviation/City of Chicago
Concrete mast with steel outriggers at perimeter
Clear glass infill panels

The new control tower is the landmark of O'Hare International Airport, providing a highly visible point of orientation in the airport landscape.

The core of the tower is a concrete column which contains the elevator, cables, and technical equipment, with the staircase wrapped around it. The surrounding steel support structure is connected to the core by horizontal posts, and stayed to the foundations. A glass curtain covers the steel elements, creating a shape that reflects the functions of the tower.

During the day, the shape of the tower is dictated by the glass surfaces, transparency and reflection creating an interesting dialogue. At night, artificial lighting creates depth and transforms the tower into a luminous object—a beacon for O'Hare.

1 Concept sketches
2 View from roadway

Kuala Lumpur City Center 1

Design 1991
Kuala Lumpur, Malaysia
Seri Kuda Sdn. Bhd.
8,000,000 square feet
Structural steel, glass and metal curtain wall

The design for the Kuala Lumpur City Center, sited at the former Royal Racecourse, is an attempt to re-examine the planning of dense urban multi-use centers. The development is the initial phase of the Kuala Lumpur City Center Master Plan.

The plan includes three office towers, a retail block and a hotel organized along a wide "main street", or spine, identified by its undulating roof structure. The retail is developed as a series of arcades and town squares emerging from and connecting to the main street.

The 95-story Petronus Tower and a smaller 50-story office slab front onto the "main street". A third office tower, 85 stories in height, is located along Jalan Ampang adjacent to the proposed Civic Center. The Convention Hotel is located to the south of the Petronus Tower. Each building has a distinct image which, through its technical features and use of color, establishes a language and builds a relationship with the larger urban context.

1   Interplay of individual tower element, hotel and retail

Barnett Center

Design/Completion 1988/1990
Jacksonville, Florida
Paragon Group Inc.
1,000,000 square feet
Cast-in-place reinforced concrete frame
Color-coated aluminum curtain wall system with reflective blue glass and Fjord blue granite

The brief for Barnett Center called for a soaring sculpture reaching a new height for Jacksonville, Florida. The building was designed as an obelisk, a rich traditional architectural form symbolizing achievement, power, glory, and victory. It is a meaningful symbol of the position of Barnett Bank within the financial community. Its elegant exterior treatment of horizontal and vertical patterns of blue-gray granite with silver mullions and blue tinted glass expresses the timelessness of an established financial institution.

The 42-story tower contains 710,000 square feet of office space, as well as parking for 654 cars, a spacious lobby, and a grand banking hall. The building is surrounded by a landscaped plaza giving access to ground floor retail and banking functions and the two-story lobby.

1 Concept sketches
2 Entrance
3 An obelisk on the Jacksonville skyline

Yokohama Waterfront MM21 Project

Design 1990
Yokohama, Japan
Mitsui & Co.
Associate Architect: AAS Associates International Co.
4,500,000 square feet
Tower portions steel moment connected frame base; steel moment connected frame
Painted aluminum panel and structure enclosure with clear and patterned fritted glass

The Yokohama Waterfront Project in the Minato Mirai District contemplates the extension of the city center to establish Yokohama as Japan's second major metropolis in the international marketplace. The complex provides offices, hotels, residential development, the Yokohama Design Port, retail, entertainment, restaurants, a symphony hall, and parking.

Architecturally, the scheme is a composition of bays and towers connected by a liner above a base. The towers, containing the building cores, flank the streets and denote major entries into the retail precincts. Between these towers are the offices, hotels, and residences. The base is trisected by two atria in the east–west direction, providing a city–water connection. It is bisected in the north–south direction by the Queen Mall. The programmatic elements are situated under the wing-like roof, creating a public terrace level between the roof of the individual elements and the wing.

1. Concept sketch
2. Ground-floor plan
3. South-east elevation
4. View from the east

Yokohama Waterfront MM21 Project 87

Tokyo Teleport Town

Design 1990
Tokyo, Japan
Mitsui Real Estate/Kajima Corporation
Associate Architect: Kajima Corporation
900,000 square feet
Structural steel frame with exposed bracing
Glass curtain wall and granite paving

The Tokyo Teleport Town extends the Tokyo metropolis onto land reclaimed from Tokyo Bay. The site borders a central promenade that is terminated by the Telecom Center Building.

The scheme comprises two nearly identical towers. By turning one tower 45° towards the other, the composition assumes a certain strength which relates to the Telecom Center yet holds its own. The siting of the two buildings also resolves the symmetrical and asymmetrical qualities of the site. The buildings are simple in form and express their refinement through meticulous detailing. The orthogonal tower is clad in blue glass while the rotated tower is clad in green glass, avoiding the obvious solution of two identical towers.

The towers are positioned on a raised podium which unifies the space between them, establishes a common entry to the offices and amenities, and provides a special space for outdoor activities. The space between the buildings is further defined by a glass roof supported by steel trusses at the thirteenth floor.

1 Site plan
2 Typical floor plans
3 Interplay of rotated buildings
4 Lobby
5 Buildings and plaza elements

Tokyo Teleport Town 89

425 Lexington Avenue

Design/Completion 1985/1989
New York, New York
Olympia & York Equity Corporation
565,000 square feet
Steel frame, metal deck
Aluminum curtain wall with green and buff granite, insulated vision glass and fritted spandrel glass

The project site occupies a full-block frontage between 43rd and 44th Streets along the eastern side of Lexington Avenue in midtown Manhattan. The features of the landmark Chrysler Building, situated directly across 43rd Street to the south, had a decisive influence on the design concept.

The building typology is an innovative variation on the "architectural column". The plan of the tower is a rectangle with strongly chamfered corners, rising from a stepped and similarly chamfered base. The tower top, like the capital of a column, hovers over the shaft and base and, in a contrasting gesture, flares outward at the same height at which the Chrysler tower steps inward.

The main entrance, on Lexington Avenue, is bounded by retail shopfronts. This entrance is the dominant recess in the streetwall, and leads directly to a "grand salon" type lobby with a coffered, luminous ceiling.

1   Ground-floor plan
2   Lexington Avenue entrance with Chrysler Building
3   Lobby
4   Curtain wall top detail

4

750 Lexington Avenue

Design/Completion 1984/1989
New York, New York
Cohen Brothers
365,000 square feet
Steel structure
Painted aluminum mullions with tinted and reflective glass; blue pearl granite spandrels and base

750 Lexington Avenue is a 30-story office tower occupying a key site within midtown Manhattan. It is directly on top of a major subway station, and major improvements to the subway entrances are included as part of the project.

The design involves the interlocking of two geometric volumes: an inner cylinder is wrapped by an outer volume which changes its configuration from a rectangle to a polygon based on 45° geometry. The cylinder projects from this form at the top, and also on Lexington Avenue to form a giant bay window. The stepped top, with its projecting light feature, gives the building an interesting profile and promotes recognition.

On the ground floor along Lexington Avenue the retail frontage extends beyond the outline of the tower to reinforce streetwall continuity and provide retail exposure. Along the western property line, similar extensions serve as office building entry points.

1 Concept sketches
2 Stepped top
3 City context
4 Interlocking skin elements
5 Streetscape showing retail

750 Lexington Avenue 93

Cityspire

Design/Completion 1984/1989
New York, New York
West 56th Street Associates
842,000 square feet
High strength poured-in-place concrete
Tinted vision glass, vertical and horizontal granite panels, painted aluminum mullions, painted steel plate ribs and aluminum fins at the dome

Situated at the northern edge of New York City's historic Broadway Theater District, the Cityspire rises as one of Manhattan's tallest and most prominent residential/mixed-use towers.

The site is adjacent to the recently landmark-designated City Center Theater of Music and Drama. A transfer of unused development rights above the City Center Theater enabled this mid-block project to reach a height of approximately 70 stories, with 353 luxury condominium units surmounting 23 stories of speculative office space and retail.

Careful attention to scale and materials at the new tower's base attempts to relate the 56th Street facade to its existing neighbor. Rising out of this base in a series of three setbacks is a stone-clad octagonal shaft with lateral wings of glass projecting to the east and west. These wings ultimately terminate at the sixty-first floor, releasing an 80-foot diameter omni-directional tower with copper dome into the skyline.

1 Omni-directional tower with copper dome

Project J (1, 2, 3)

Design 1989
Chicago, Illinois
Howard Ecker & Co.
PJ-1/PJ-2: 600,000 square feet
PJ-3: 400,000 square feet
Slip form concrete core
Poured-in-place column and slab, stone and aluminum skin

These projects represent similar concepts developed for a number of sites and sizes.

PJ-1 is an office building that develops from the overlapping and integration of multiple architectural elements, and the influences of the program, the neighborhood, and current technology.

Typologically the building is a corner building that responds to the urban situation of the city to the south and the lake to the east. The corner is clearly articulated as a round bay with a recessed entry at street level and full circular floors at the building top.

PJ-2 is an office building with retail and parking, located on the near north side of Chicago. The goal was to create a state-of-the-art building of superior quality to attract first-rate tenants. PJ-3 was developed for an alternative site north of the river, and is essentially a downscaling of PJ-2 in anticipation of reduced market conditions, while still being a highly visible building.

1   Project J-1
2   Project J-2
3   Project J-3: concept sketches

Wilshire/Westwood

Design/Completion 1984/1988
Los Angeles, California
Platt Corporation
230,000 square feet
Ductile steel moment frame
Color-coated aluminum window wall system with reflective gray glass;
Kasota limestone, granite on strong back truss system

The building is located along a section of Wilshire Boulevard lined by typical high-rise development. The form of these buildings is reduced to a slab, square or octagon, with the skin representing the horizontal layering of office floors, the verticality of the columns, or the structural bays. The design of this project attempts to collage these "fragments" of the urban scene into a new form. A rectangular slab with sloping and stepped ends is combined with two octagonal towers that read as giant columns. A combination of glass and stone finishes accentuate the setbacks and create a capital-like top.

At the street level, the building abuts the property lines with commercial uses, creating an arcaded appearance. A large octagonal public reception space at the corner serves as a monumental entry. The remainder of the site has been landscaped as a public park to make the transition to the residential scale to the south.

1   Concept sketches
2   Site plan
3   Wilshire/Midvale elevation

3

4 Car entrance
5 Typical floor plans
6 Midvale elevation
7 Lobby

5

6

7

Wilshire/Westwood 99

1111 Brickell Avenue

Design 1988
Miami, Florida
Brickell Associates
1,740,000 square feet
Steel and concrete structure
Glass and aluminum curtain wall

1111 Brickell Avenue is a mixed-use complex consisting of two high-rise towers sitting on a base fronting a public plaza. One tower is exclusively for office use. The upper portion of the second tower provides 230 hotel rooms and associated public areas, with office space on the floors below. The base houses the entry lobbies for the office and hotel functions; a two-level retail arcade; parking for 1,150 cars; and building services.

Each tower is sculptured differently to give it an identifiable form. The tower facing towards the south-west corner of Brickell Avenue has a cantilevered, semi-circular form that provides panoramic views. The second tower has two cantilevered rectangular bays that meet in a re-entrant corner facing Brickell Avenue. The two towers and the base are tied together by a two-story, 30-foot grid of white marble or granite, with black granite at the street level and between the towers.

1   South elevation
2   View from the south-west
3   West elevation

The North Loop Block 37

Design 1988
Chicago, Illinois
FJV Venture
2,300,000 square feet
Concrete structure
Granite and glass curtain wall

Ambitious in scale as well as intent, this project confirms the latent vitality of Chicago's North Loop, providing a vision of the future for this part of the city. The project is conceived as a full-block development consisting of 300,000 square feet of retail and two office towers, organized along a pedestrian arcade.

The backbone of the project is the 320-foot four-story retail arcade with central rotunda, which connects the office population to the west with existing retail activities to the east. It offers a protected urban space accessible only to pedestrians, and provides connections between essential points of origin and destination.

North and south of the arcade, the two office towers rise above the retail activities providing 1.9 million square feet of office space. Each building has a separate corner entry along Dearborn Street, while the second-story lobbies are linked directly to the arcade.

1 Dearborn Street with Civic Center Plaza
2 State Street
3 Ground-floor plan

Oakbrook Terrace Tower

Design/Completion 1985/1987
Oakbrook Terrace, Illinois
Miglin Beitler Inc.
714,000 square feet
Reinforced concrete core and steel frame
Aluminum and glass curtain wall; terrazzo floors with marble cladding in lobby

The Oakbrook Terrace Tower provides 663,000 square feet of office space in a 29-story tower. The building is sited on 16 acres in the suburb of Oakbrook Terrace approximately 25 miles west of Chicago.

The tower is conceived as an octagon in plan, with emphasis on the orthogonal planes. The four diagonal faces employ a horizontal expression that, when played against the vertical, provides a high level of visual interest from the surrounding road network. This play of horizontal and vertical generates the tower's top which is the building's signature.

The tower provides typical floors of 23,800 square feet. The twenty-ninth floor contains an additional mezzanine, providing a unique opportunity for a tenant who requires a distinct identity. The lobby atria reinforce the ceremonial aspects of the design. A restaurant is located at the ground floor, while the lower level contains a health club as well as parking for 200 cars.

1 Site plan
2 Vertical entrance facade with horizontal chamfered corners
3 Entrance
4 Lobby
5 Elevator lobby

2
3
4
5

Oakbrook Terrace Tower 103

One Liberty Place

Design/Completion 1984/1987
Philadelphia, Pennsylvania
Rouse Associates
1,100,000 square feet
Steel frame and composite deck
Fluoropolymer-coated aluminum curtain wall with reflective glass, polished and honed granite

The Liberty Place project occupies a prime block in central Philadelphia, assembled through the closing of two streets. One Liberty Place is the first phase of the project, sited on the corner of 17th and Market Streets, and contains 61 stories of office space. Special high-rise zoning allows the project to exceed the 491-foot height limit of William Penn's statue on top of the Philadelphia City Hall.

The tower itself is square with re-entrant corners. The shift in plane between the building's shaft and the corners emphasizes the location of eight "super columns" which are tied with outriggers to the building's braced central core at intermittent floor levels. This "outrigger/super column" structure permits greater flexibility and openness for office space and ground-floor retail than the conventional "tube" system.

From the base, which is clad in stone, the amount of glass increases until the top is totally sheathed in glass.

1 Concept sketches
2 Cityscape
3 Overall view: One Liberty Place
4 Liberty Place phases I and II

2

3

4

One Liberty Place 105

5

6

7

5 Entrance
6 Side entrance
7 Streetscape with storefronts
8 Lobby

Northwestern Atrium Center

Design/Completion 1984/1987
Chicago, Illinois
Tishman Midwest Management Corp.
1,600,000 square feet
Braced perimeter steel frame; atrium framing of lightweight steel trusses
Exterior tube aluminum curtain wall with infill of reflective silver, reflective blue, and black-tinted glass

The Northwestern Atrium Center Project is a combined commuter terminal and office building complex replacing the existing Chicago and Northwestern Train Station. The building forms a major gateway between the station and Madison Street, removing the "Chinese Wall" effect of the existing station on the growth of the central business district.

A continuous arcade along Madison Street leads to a sequence of multi-story atria which enhance commuter traffic flow to the train platform. The atrium spaces bring light to the inside without the penalty of heat loss or gain.

On street and track levels, 85,000 square feet of terminal facilities serve the requirements of a modern commuter station. The office tower is served from a skylobby one floor above track level. The form of the tower reflects the symmetry of the scheme and the varying floor sizes. Its smooth, streamlined curves create a shape which appropriately symbolizes the image of trains.

1 Ground-floor plan
2 Typical floor plan
3 South facade
4 Roll-back entrance arcade
5 South atrium

Northwestern Atrium Center

6 North atrium passenger train arrival/waiting area
7 South entrance atrium/retail
8 Escalator to third-floor skylobby
9 Entrance gateway
10 North elevation with passenger train sheds

362 West Street

Design/Completion 1983/1986
Durban, South Africa
Anglo-American Properties
Associate Architect: Stauch Vorster + Partners
22,000 square feet
Tower: concrete frame with aluminum and glass curtain wall
Arcade: exposed steel frame with glass curtain wall

362 West Street is a mixed-use development containing 231,400 square feet of office space in a 24-story tower and 32,300 square feet of retail space in a 2-story base structure. The development provides a continuation of the lively character of the existing streetscape, with shopfronts along the sidewalks as well as retail arcades at mid-block.

The tower is a geometric configuration of two concentric octagons. The outer form spirals about the inner form which culminates in a steep spire housing microwave and communications equipment. A landscaped roof terrace is provided at each floor level, introducing a natural element and providing vistas over the bay and the Indian Ocean.

The physical configuration of this design provides an interesting alternative to the typical office building of identical stacked floors, with varying amounts of floorspace provided at each level.

1–2 Concept sketches
3 Typical floor plan
4 Retail arcade/pedestrian way
5 Outer and inner octagons with terraces

3   SEVENTH FLOOR

4

5

362 West Street

Park Avenue Tower

Design/Completion 1982/1986
New York, New York
Park Tower Realty
480,000 square feet
Steel frame with metal deck composite floor construction
Aluminum and glass curtain wall with granite panels glazed into the curtain wall framing system

The project occupies a through-block site connecting 55th and 56th Streets between Park and Madison Avenues in mid-town Manhattan. Two distinguished corporate neighbors are the high-rise headquarters buildings for ATT and IBM.

The dominant image projected by the building is that of a monumental granite and glass obelisk. This form resulted from the programmatic requirement for variable floor sizes together with the converging sky exposure curves. The north and south facades of the tower slope inwards eventually converging with the vertical east–west facades to form a perfect 110-foot square at the top. The sloping and chamfered tower walls incorporate the characteristic New York setback in three tiers concealed within the flush streamline taper of the overall form.

The building contains 35 office floors ranging in size from 17,000 gross square feet in the base to an average of 13,500 square feet in the tapering floors of the tower. An urban plaza is located along the entire site frontage of 55th Street.

1 View from Park Avenue
2 Typical floor plan
3 Entrance
4 Chamfered corner/setback
5 Elevator lobby

Park Avenue Tower 115

Metro West

Design/Completion 1984/1986
Naperville, Illinois
Westminister Corporation
232,000 square feet
Steel frame structure
Color-coated unitized curtain wall system with reflective gray glass and flamed Luna Pearl light gray granite

Metro West is a 10-story speculative office building located in an office/research park west of metropolitan Chicago. The project consists of two buildings in phased development linked by an enclosed atrium structure. The design establishes a raised landscaped podium for the base of the integrated structures.

The cubic forms of the office buildings are related at a 45° angle on the axis of the platform area. The curvilinear atrium structure is suspended from the opposing faces of the buildings and becomes an independent geometry, linking the buildings with an enclosed space which is polygonal in plan and undulating in elevation.

The office building facade consists of inner and outer walls separated by a series of 15-foot-wide terraces which step up the building along a diagonal. The diagonal offset in plan creates four additional corner offices on each floor, each with an adjoining terrace.

1 Entrance with terraces
2 View from the south-west
3 Typical floor plan
4 Punched window within granite wall

2

3

4

Metro West 117

South Ferry Plaza

Design 1986
New York, New York
Olympia & York Equity Corporation
1,200,000 square feet
Steel frame with metal deck
Aluminum and glass curtain wall

Envisioned as a symbolic entry to New York City, the South Ferry Plaza Project transforms a confused traffic nexus into a dramatic sequence of public spaces that culminates in a 50-story tower marking the juncture of water and land transit.

The project is situated at the southern tip of Manhattan along the edge of the East River. Its public components include a new ferry terminal for the Staten Island Ferry, an observation plaza, and the Museum of Maritime History, all gathered beneath the welcoming arches of the commercial office tower. Monumental and maritime influences combine in the form of a lighthouse or harbor beacon that confidently marks Manhattan's prow.

The tower shaft rises out of a triangular base that gracefully transforms its three-sided plan into a hexagon. Great arches at the tower base channel gravity loads to three points straddling existing subway lines, Battery Park underpass, ferry slips and related terminal spaces, thus allowing virtually obstacle-free circulation space at grade.

1 Section with Staten Island Ferry facilities
2 Cityscape

Columbus Circle

Design 1985
New York, New York
Trump Organization
2,100,000 square feet
Steel frame/metal deck
Glass and aluminum curtain wall

The development site, located on Columbus Circle between 58th and 60th Streets, is currently occupied by the New York Coliseum. The project is envisaged as a multi-use complex of office, hotel and residential spaces.

The base structure contains retail space and new subway entrances. Office and residential entries are located at 58th Street, with additional office and hotel entries at 60th Street. Five floors of loft-type office space are also provided.

The tower is conceived as a segmented hollow octagonal tube 1,275 feet in height. A 230-foot-high slot is provided to reinforce the 59th Street view corridor. The tower is set back at skylobby level, 300 feet above grade. This level houses the main residential and hotel lobbies. The remainder of the tower terraces upwards in a spiralling configuration, commanding views of Central Park and the Hudson River.

1   View from Central Park

Bank of Southwest Tower

Design 1985
Houston, Texas
Century Development Corporation
Associate Architects: Lloyd Jones Brewer Associates
2,500,000 square feet
Composite steel and concrete structural system; eight perimeter "super columns" tied to concrete core with steel diagonals
Vertical aluminum tube mullions with reflective glass panels, stone spandrels with horizontal glass infill at corners

The design for the Bank of Southwest Tower juxtaposes the spirit and richness of past forms with present-day technique and materials. The obelisk, rotated on the site, is the basic formal generator of the design. The facades of the obelisk are framed by the major columns. The shift which occurs at these columns between the building's sloped and stepped facades reinforces the structure as load-bearing, and the nature of the skin as infill.

The surfaces of the building are treated in different combinations of granite, aluminum and glass, projecting an institutional and timeless character. The base is of granite to emphasize its strength and solidity, and uses classical forms in its detailing for the triangular arches and gables. The eight columns are faced with stone and merge with the stone gables at the top of the building.

1 Site plan
2 Typical floor plan
3 Rotated obelisk on city skyline

3

Bank of Southwest Tower 121

11 Diagonal Street

Design/Completion 1981/1984
Johannesburg, South Africa
Anglo American Properties
Associate Architect: Louis Karol Architects
350,000 square feet
Concrete structure
Double wall skin, blue and silver reflective glass with red steel exposed frames supporting exterior curtain wall

The site for this building is a full block in an area known as Newtown adjacent to the central business district of Johannesburg. The building takes the form of a diamond, both in reference to the diamond industry association of the developer's parent company, and to conform to the city's sloping height restrictions.

The building enclosure consists of a double skin. The inner wall is 50 per cent glass in a continuous strip, butt-jointed and silicone-sealed. This allows complete flexibility in locating interior partitions along the exterior wall. The space between the inner and outer walls provides an environmental buffer which is naturally ventilated. The exterior wall of reflective glass in aluminum frames acts as a sun shade, reducing solar gain.

1 Site plan
2 Entrance
3 Cityscape
4 Lobby
5 Front elevation

11 Diagonal Street 123

Chicago Board of Trade Addition

Design/Completion 1978/1982
Chicago, Illinois
Chicago Board of Trade Joint Venture
Architects: Shaw and Associates; Swanke Hayden Connell Architects
584,000 square feet
Steel frame supporting two-story-high trusses over trading floor; glass roof supported on steel trusses
Aluminum curtain wall grid module, silver reflective vision/spandrel glass in combination with dark gray vision/spandrel glass and limestone veneer

The building provides 584,000 gross square feet for the Chicago Board of Trade, including a new trading floor and support spaces as well as office space for exchange members and staff. The addition is designed to function with the existing building as one unit.

The addition responds functionally and formally to the existing Art Deco landmark structure. The first 12 floors, housing the trading floor and support activities, correspond to similar spaces in the existing structure. Above this level, office floors are designed as U-shaped spaces around a central atrium which adjoins the existing structure. To provide the required trading floor area, the building projects 20 feet beyond the existing structure, creating a covered pedestrian arcade at street level.

A glass skin wraps the highly articulated planes of the wall and the roof.

1   Ground-floor plan
2   View from the south-west
3   Twelfth floor atrium

One South Wacker

Design/Completion 1979/1982
Chicago, Illinois
Metropolitan Structures/Harvey Walken & Co.
1,280,000 square feet
Reinforced concrete structure
Aluminum and glass curtain wall; terrazzo floors with marble and glass lobby

This is essentially an adaption of the typical office tower of the 1920s to today's standards and requirements. The concept of the building is based on providing very large floor areas, ranging from 25,000 to 38,000 gross square feet. The building is set back twice, giving three typical floor areas. Three-story atriums located above and below the setbacks create U-shaped floor areas and thus reduce the depth of the lease-span and increase the perimeter and daylight exposure.

At the ground floor the atrium extends into a multi-level commercial galleria which serves as a civilized public amenity, providing a through-way between the Wacker and Madison entrances to the building. Commercial functions are kept to the exterior, in keeping with the character of the adjacent streetscape.

1   Ground-floor plan
2   Lobby
3   Looking south on Wacker Drive
4   Wacker Drive elevation at night
5   City context with Chicago River
6   Entrance

3

4

5

6

One South Wacker 127

Xerox Centre

Design/Completion 1978/1980
Chicago, Illinois
Romanek-Golub
880,000 square feet
Reinforced concrete cast-in-place
Unitized aluminum panel and insulated glass system

The building's typology is that of an "infill building on a corner". Like the existing buildings in the block, it extends to the property line along Monroe Street and is set back on Dearborn, continuing the landscaped promenade established by the First National Bank. It is also set back at Marble Court to provide light and views on the lower levels. The building curves at the corner to make the transition between its two sides and symbolically suggest its treatment as a single front. At the ground floor the curved wall continues to form recessed entries; at the roof it makes the transition to the mechanical penthouse.

Above the height of the existing structures on Monroe Street, the building slopes to assume its tower configuration. This provides a strong continuity between old and new, and is a break with the concept of a "freestanding tower" on a plaza.

1 Site plan
2 Transition of facades at corner
3 Overall view from the north-east

Selected and Current Works

Urban Block Buildings

132	Ku-Damm 70
136	Pallas Office Building
142	Charlemagne
143	Principal Mutual Life Insurance Company
144	Stralauer Platz 35
148	Sony Center, Berlin
150	Victoria Versicherungsgesellshaft
152	Ku-Damm 119
154	Mannheimer Lebensversicherung Headquarters
158	Augustinerhof-Nuernberg
160	Europa-Haus
161	Lufthansa Corporate Headquarters
162	Harold Washington Library Center Competition
163	First & Broadway Los Angeles Civic Center
164	State of Illinois Center
168	Shand Morahan Corporate Headquarters
170	First Source Center

Ku-Damm 70

Design/Completion 1988/1994
Berlin, Germany
Euwo Unternehmensgruppe
12,000 square feet
Steel floors hung with rods from steel trusses supported by a concrete core
Curtain wall of fritted glass, aluminum mullions and aluminum panels

This is the first building of a series on Ku-Damm. It is an urban repair project, covering the end of a building exposed through insensitive and destructive street planning in the 1950s. In its attitude the building is an urban intervention against the mediocrity of the new city along the Ku-Damm, evoking nostalgia for the lost Berlin tradition.

Due to an available site width of only 10 feet, the building was allowed to be cantilevered over the sidewalk on Ku-Damm and Lewishamstrasse, and to exceed the height of the adjacent building. This makes the building a marker on Ku-Damm, an image reinforced by its knife-like plan configuration and its steel mast with sign.

The steel floors are hung from the 10-foot-wide concrete service core. Cladding is of an all-glass skin, accentuated by the hangers and alternating floors. The glass is fritted to create different transparencies in response to the view conditions from the inside, resulting in a decorative pattern within this strong construct.

1

1   Ku-Damm elevation
2   Concept sketches
3   Plans and section
4   Knife-like plan with mast
5   Steel mast detail/sign creating a symbol on Ku-Damm

Ku-Damm 70 133

6–9 Curtain wall details with fritted patterned glass
10 Knife-like plan with steel mast

6

7

8

9

10

Pallas Office Building

Design/Completion 1989/1994
Stuttgart, Germany
IGEPA Industrie und Gewerbepark Bautraeger
600,000 square feet
Concrete structure
Curtain wall of light and dark granite, glass and aluminum

The site for this project is located in a suburb of Stuttgart which is in transition from light industry to office and service uses. The existing cityscape presents a random collection of buildings based primarily on industrial prerogatives.

The building mass uses the clearly articulated streetwalls of the traditional European city block to establish a strong exterior presence and reveal a new interior urban space. The building extends to the boundary on all sides, defining a solid block with rounded corners. A primary gate facing the main train station provides automobile access to the three main lobbies. Secondary gates at the corners of the courtyard transform the simple wall masses into tower elements.

In the courtyard stand three glass wedges set into black granite walls, defining the building's main entrances. At the base of the wedges are high stone arcades leading to the main lobbies.

1 Site/ground-floor plan
2 Entrance gate
3 City block
4 Tower element
5 Granite wall and arcade

Pallas Office Building 137

6

7

8

6   Courtyard
7   Glass wedges
8   Entrance drive
9   Secondary gate
10 Punched granite wall
11 Glass wall
12 Entrance gate

Pallas Office Building

13 Arcade
14 Lobby arcade
15 Elevator corridor
16 Lobby

14

15

16

Pallas Office Building   141

Charlemagne

Design/Completion 1994/1997
Brussels, Belgium
Etudes et Investissements Immobiliers, SA/NV
Associate Architect: ARC, SA Architectes
614,000 square feet
Steel structure, glass bay point and screen wall additions
Clear and patterned fritted glass with printed aluminum mullions; stone-clad base with button-glazed lobby front

The Charlemagne project is an addition and remodeling of the existing Charlemagne building at Rue de la Loi 170, Brussels. Constructed in 1968, this 15-story Y-shaped building is situated on a three-story parking base which is exposed at the Rue du Taciturne due to the slope of the site. The existing building contains 431,733 square feet of office space above grade.

This project modifies the existing building in several ways. A 5.5-foot addition wraps the existing Y, forming a 71-foot tri-span office plan. The ends of the east and west wings are extended to the site boundary. Two curved winter gardens fill the void between the three wings of the Y. The center wing is cut back to unify the curved shape of the two winter gardens. The top of the parking base is transformed into a raised urban garden terrace accessible from the two winter gardens.

1 Curved winter garden facade
2 Sun-shade screen wall on Rue de la Loi

Principal Mutual Life Insurance Company

Design/Completion 1993/1995
Des Moines, Iowa
Principal Mutual Life Insurance Company
518,000 square feet
Structural steel frame with composite deck
Clear and patterned spandrel glass, fluoropolymer-coated aluminum panels, limestone cladding

The project program called for 456,650 gross square feet of new office space to be developed on the site in downtown Des Moines. The plan creates a public plaza between the new building, at the north end of the site, and Corporate Square to the south, linking the two with a public skywalk.

The building is developed on a broad footprint at the north end of the site. The large floor plates enable the mass of the building to be reduced in height and conform to the scale of the immediate context. The plan of the building can be interpreted as a long, linear element which has been "folded up" to fit the site, and simultaneously to define the street spaces to the north, east, and west.

In one interpretation, the building becomes a "wall" determining the north edge of the plaza; in another sense, the building becomes a giant "gateway" linking areas to the north and south.

1 Folded linear footprint of building with wall and gate
2 Public plaza connecting the new building with existing corporate offices

Principal Mutual Life Insurance Company 143

Stralauer Platz 35

Design/Completion 1993/1997
Berlin, Germany
OPUS Entwicklungsgesellschaft
468,000 square feet
Placed concrete
White granite with gray granite base, patterned fritted glass cable net wall structures, coated steel and aluminum sun shades and Krone

Occupying a site formerly bisected by the Berlin Wall, the building is to be read as a permeable form rather than as a volume constructed of edges.

The high plaza is framed by two buildings, a moderate five-story structure and a stepped 15-story building addressing the park and corner. The open plaza extends the Stralauer Platz as the main entry to the building complex. A river promenade is created by lowering the grade along the constant-level riverfront. As future development continues, a wide pedestrian path will extend along the riverfront park.

The Spree stair connects the two levels. Incorporating both steps and landscaped terracing, the stair will become the type of informal gathering place which characterizes the habitable city. The winter garden, a high vertical space, terminates the expanse of the parklands to the east. The enclosed area mitigates the solar exposure on this face of the project and provides an extended comfort zone to cafe functions at the park's edge.

1 Concept sketch
2 Site plan
3 Winter garden
4 Context

Stralauer Platz 35 145

5

6

7

5   Stepped 15-story tower
6   River promenade
7   Pedestrian path
8   Winter garden
9   River view

Stralauer Platz 35   147

Sony Center, Berlin

Design/Completion 1993/1999
Berlin, Germany
Sony Corporation
1,670,000 square feet
Reinforced concrete and steel frame
Naturally ventilated glass and aluminum curtain wall

The program for the Sony Center required spectacular office headquarters, a cinema and cultural complex, retail, a hotel, apartments, and parking.

The buildings are shaped to respond to the urban situations at the perimeter, such as the Potsdamer Platz, the boulevard of the Potsdamer Strasse, the Kemper Platz and the Bellevue-Park. Materials used on the facades are stone, metal and glass in different combinations and configurations which respond to each building's use and form.

The attic floors of the Sony headquarters frame a giant inward-sloping "show window", overlayed with a monumental order of columns, providing views into the atrium and exhibition space. At the Filmhaus a "screen" projects from its gridded and framed glass facade. The larger-scale elements of "show window" and "screen" respond to the faster movements along the Entlastungs Strasse and to the solitary buildings of the Kulturforum.

1 Axonometric
2 Bellevue Strasse elevation
3 Entlastungs Strasse/Potsdamer Strasse
4–7 Concept sketches

Sony Center, Berlin 149

Victoria Versicherungsgesellschaft

Design/Completion 1992/1997
Berlin, Germany
Victoria Versicherungsgesellschaft
823,400 square feet
Placed concrete, steel and aluminum, and glass roofs and canopies
Structural glazing system with clear and patterned fritted vision glass and spandrel glass

Based on a partially realized plan of 1957, the Victoria Project concludes the redevelopment of Berlin at the corner of the Kurfuerstendamm and Joachimstalerstrasse. Befitting the status of the Kurfuerstendamm as one of Berlin's pre-eminent streets, the new Victoria building emphasizes the defining eight-story high cornice at the streetwall. Except for the minor segment of retail development to be removed, the existing buildings will be upgraded. The existing eight-story Victoria building will be provided with a new, more accessible and gracious entrance.

The project deviates from the originally planned scheme by including over 100 residential units. The apartments are located away from the busy main streets at the north-west quadrant of the site. Retail functions will be provided at all newly constructed grade-level areas and some second-level areas. Existing retail areas will be upgraded.

1 City context
2 Passageway from Kantsrasse
3 Kurfuerstendamm/Joachimstalerstrasse
4 Ground-floor/site plan
5 Rendering from Kurfuerstendamm/Joachimstalerstrasse

Victoria Versicherungsgesellschaft

Ku-Damm 119

Design/Completion 1988/1995
Berlin, Germany
Athena Grundstuecks AG; Vebau GmbH Frankfurt/Berlin
150,000 square feet
Poured-in-place reinforced concrete
Panelized aluminum/glass curtain wall with green or gray tinted glass, patterned spandrel glass and painted aluminum panels; piers and base black granite

This building completes a partially existing block configuration. It adjusts to the irregular site with rounded corners acting like hinges, and steps down from eight floors to five floors. At the corners the building has special features, such as projecting glass bays, steel brows and steel masts, which reflect features of the historic city in a new way.

The linear nature of the building is reinforced through a banded aluminum and glass facade, which is replaced by glass at the two upper floors to correspond to the lower cornice height of the adjacent buildings. The building has a center core configuration allowing for flexible leasing arrangements and multiple-tenant use. Below grade are 180 parking spaces, and service and technical areas.

A landscaped courtyard provides accessible urban open space, offering additional urban linkages within this city quarter.

1 Concept sketches
2 Floor plan
3 Round corner/entrance
4 Banded curtain wall
5 Linear building expressing rounded corners/entrance

3

4

5

Ku-Damm 119

Mannheimer Lebensversicherung Headquarters

Design/Completion 1988/1992
Mannheim, Germany
Mannheimer Lebensversicherung AG
236,000 square feet
Concrete structure, steel brow
Curtain wall of glass, blue pearl stone and aluminum

The brief required 150,000 square feet of office space (open-plan or single offices) to be used by the client and leased to tenants, as well as a cafeteria and parking for 280 cars.

Driving from the autobahn into Mannheim, the site is at the entrance to the inner city, at the beginning of the Augusta-Anlage—one of the most beautiful avenues in Germany. The design gives maximum presence to the building's corner site, guiding movement down the boulevard with an elegant curving gesture. The building form has a maximum height of 14 stories, accentuated by a cantilevered steel top, at the corner of the Augusta-Anlage. Moving along the boulevard towards the inner city, the building steps down into a series of two-story outdoor terraces to a typical height of four stories.

The ground floor contains the entrance lobby, dining rooms and an employee cafeteria that extends out into the landscaped courtyard in a gently curved form.

1. Site/ground-floor plan
2. North elevation
3. Landscaped courtyard
4. Building presence entering Mannheim
5. Cantilevered brow
6. Entrance

Mannheimer Lebensversicherung Headquarters 155

7 Office corridor
8 Private office
9 Lobby
10 Cafeteria
11 Kneipe

9

10

11

Mannheimer Lebensversicherung Headquarters 157

Augustinerhof-Nuernberg

Design/Completion 1990/1997
Nuernberg, Germany
DHF Bautraegergesellschaft
165,000 square feet
Concrete structure
Stone facade with punched window openings; glass and steel bays with painted aluminum mullion system; suspended and button-glazed galleria roof and retail bays

The goal of the design is to create a public covered passage between Winklerstrasse and Karlstrasse as a connection to the "Hauptmarkt". The different uses are stacked in a logical way: parking for 240 cars in two below-grade parking levels; food court and loading in the first below-grade level; retail and access to office, hotel and residential functions on the ground floor; and retail on the mezzanine level. On the first through fifth floors are located the 152-room hotel, offices, and residential use along the Augustinerstrasse.

1

1   Concept sketches
2   Entrance
3   Site/floor plan
4   Pedestrian passageway

Augustinerhof-Nuernberg 159

Europa-Haus

Design 1992
Frankfurt, Germany
SkanInvest
1,094,170 square feet
Placed concrete; steel and glass galleria roof
Coated aluminum supergrid, tinted low-E glass and patterned fritted glass in painted aluminum mullion system; textured aluminum panel system

The design for Europa-Haus works within the typology of the low block-type structures of the European city. The building becomes an urban event and creates public open spaces and linkages in a city quarter which is presently devoid of those. Here, however, the typical block-type is reconfigured. The interior court is opened, "publicized", and transformed into a pleasant, eventful urban passage.

The building configuration is the antithesis of the typical office tower in that the buildings follow the streets and conform to the urban character of the area. The building creates at once a "gate" towards the main street and a spacial closure to the urban open space to the east.

The differentiated building massing and its low height create a transition of scale and a compatibility with the existing surrounding structures. This is aided by the treatment of the building massing with different forms and surfaces.

1 Concept sketches
2 Urban passage "gate", creating an interior open court

Lufthansa Corporate Headquarters

Design 1990
Cologne, Germany
Lufthansa German Airlines
539,636 square feet
Placed concrete, steel framed roof and masts
Patterned fritted vision glass and metal panels

The sketches of the Lufthansa headquarters are based on a "unit-type" building with central courtyard. This configuration was chosen above other building types as it best met the design criteria.

In plan, the building is basically a number of individual buildings, connected through courtyards and bridges. This allows the most compact arrangement of offices and work spaces and the most comfortable working conditions. Individual offices and working areas can be arranged either in the middle or on the edge of the modules. The inside areas which are flooded with daylight and enhanced by planting, create a separation from the bordering areas, but also make visual communication possible.

The image of the building is characterized by the wing-shaped roof, making the association with aircraft. The aluminum cladding and hi-tech detailing heighten the expression of technology and progress.

1 Ground-floor plan
2 Overall view

Harold Washington Library Center Competition

Design 1988
Chicago, Illinois
City of Chicago Library System; Tishman Midwest
720,000 square feet
Placed concrete, steel arches at vaulted roof
Black granite, gray granite, structural glazing, gray marble, terne metal roof

The site for the Harold Washington Library Center invites a strong urban planning solution. Recognizing this, the design overcomes the barrier formed by the Loop elevated tracks. Rather than isolating the library to either north or south of Van Buren, the main part of the building is raised above the tracks.

The most public functions of the library—the museum store, the restaurant, and the bookstore—are located at street levels. The auditorium and exhibit halls are located on a more formal streetfront mezzanine, thus preserving the retail and entertainment character of State Street.

The non-secure public functions are housed on four large floors spanning Van Buren, linked to the rest of the library through a large central open space. This space acts as an internal street, organizing and unifying the various elements while providing for a soft, natural and indirect light that diffuses throughout the building.

1   Concept sketches
2   State Street elevation
3   View from the south-east

162   Harold Washington Library Center Competition

First & Broadway Los Angeles Civic Center

Design 1987
Los Angeles, California
RCI
630,000 square feet
Steel frame
Stone-clad columns, infill of aluminum grid sun shade and fritted glass

The First & Broadway development is a much-needed component in the completion of the overall concept of the Los Angeles Civic Mall.

The office building can be interpreted as "Siamese twins"— two 18-story buildings joined at the top providing a combined total of 600,000 gross square feet of office space. This unique building concept creates a monumental portal to the central plaza and a covered area for building entrances, while providing more functional, leasable floor areas.

The open spaces associated with the site are designed to respond to local criteria as well as large-scale urban issues. The siting of the building mass creates the formal urban plaza to the north. A variety of sizes and uses of open space are offered to the public: the grand central civic space; the more informal, smaller-scaled open spaces adjacent to the ground floor of the building; galleria and arcades associated with the retail; and rooftop terraces for daycare and dining.

1 Concept sketches
2 Public plaza and building with portal, showing major and minor mullion systems

State of Illinois Center

Design/Completion 1979/1985
Chicago, Illinois
State of Illinois; Capital Development Board
Joint Venture Architects: Lester B. Knight & Associates
1,150,000 square feet
24,000 square foot skylight over 160 foot diameter atrium
Structural steel frame, composite deck
Aluminum mullions with clear and reflective glass

The new State of Illinois Center responds to and reinforces existing urban patterns. Its two main components are a low block structure and a large central rotunda.

The south-east portion of the block is sliced away to form a sloped setback configuration with open space at the corner. The continuous but stepped-back west facade of the building rises from the street line to reinforce the LaSalle Street Canyon. An indentation of the skin at the lowest two floors creates a covered arcade which continues along LaSalle and Clark Streets as well as along the curved south-east wall.

The new element in the State of Illinois Center is the reading of the central space from the outside. This element of openness is continued along the curved facade by the five-story atria which follow the setbacks.

The interior rotunda space is a logical alternative to the exterior open spaces which already characterize other city plazas along the Dearborn-Clark corridor.

1. Site/ground-floor plan
2. City context/east elevation
3. Atrium

3

4

5

6

166

4   View from Clark/Randolph Streets
5   Pedestrian arcade/plaza
6   Interior atrium
7   Ground-floor atrium with retail
8   Entry gate

7

8

State of Illinois Center   167

Shand Morahan Corporate Headquarters

Design/Completion 1982/1984
Evanston, Illinois
Walken Souyoul Interests
173,000 square feet
Steel frame
Green fluoropolymer-coated aluminum curtain wall system for reflective glass, gray and black granite cladding

This is the first phase of a two-phase project for the headquarters of an international insurance underwriter. Phase I has 173,000 square feet in eight stories, Phase II has 150,000 square feet in six stories.

The building is located on the edge of the central business district. An elevated railroad embankment borders the site and creates its triangular shape.

The L-shaped building was designed to provide a building not wider than 90 feet with a maximum distance of 45 feet to a window from any point within the building. The L shape also provides an opportunity to "reach out" and provide a covered arcade for the parking side of the building as well as the side toward the commuter facilities.

The entrance is located at the corner to provide optimum access for employees using either parking or commuter facilities. Executive offices are located on the top floors and access roof terraces.

1 Concept sketches
2 Site/floor plan
3 Corner orientation with inner and outer skins
4 Chamfered end wall
5 Pedestrian arcade with punched windows in granite wall

Shand Morahan Corporate Headquarters 169

First Source Center

Design/Completion 1978/1982
South Bend, Indiana
First Source Bank; Rahn Properties; City of South Bend
490,000 square feet
Cast-in-place concrete building frame; steel joint atrium roof frame
Clear and reflective insulated glass and metal panels

First Source Center is a multi-use urban development. It occupies a whole city block next to the new Century Center and acts as a catalyst for expansion of the CBD to the north. It consists of a 150,000 square foot bank/office building (First Source Bank), a 300-room hotel, a 27,000 square foot public atrium, and a 520-car parking garage.

The various functions have been distributed to reinforce existing compatible land uses. First Bank occupies the pivotal corner towards the CBD, while the hotel is oriented towards Century Center and contains provisions for a future closed pedestrian bridge. The atrium, which includes the hotel restaurant, is situated between those structures, and parking is on two levels below grade. From the enclosed atrium, a landscaped area with convenience parking provides the visual and physical continuity to a city park to the north of the site.

1 Axonometric
2 Entrance detail
3 Front elevation
4 Atrium spine
5 Atrium entrance

First Source Center 171

Selected and Current Works

Transportation Buildings

174	Hotel Kempinski/Munich Airport Center/Walkways
190	Dearborn Station
192	Bangkok International Airport
196	Flughafen Köln/Bonn Terminal 2
200	Hyatt Regency Roissy
204	King Abdulaziz International Airport Competition
208	One America Plaza/Trolley Station
210	JFK Consolidated Terminal
214	United Airlines Terminal One Complex
220	O'Hare Rapid Transit Station

Hotel Kempinski/Munich Airport Center/Walkways

Design/Completion 1989/1994 (hotel), 1990/1996 (MAC),
  1991/1992 (walkways)
Munich, Germany
Flughafen München Gesellschaft
Hotel: 350,000 square feet
MAC: 1,000,000 square feet
Hotel: Concrete structure, steel and glass roof supported by industry steel arches, cable-stayed glass end walls
MAC: Concrete structure, cable-stayed glass and steel roof
Walkways: Metal and glass roof supported by industry steel arches on steel columns
Hotel: Glass and aluminum curtain wall
MAC: Glass and aluminum curtain wall

The master plan for the Neutral Zone of the Munich Airport foresees the development of a 3,230,000 square foot service center and 9,000 parking spaces. In contrast to the flight-related buildings of the existing terminal, the buildings of the Neutral Zone will be dedicated to service uses, entertainment, relaxation, shopping and cultural events, as well as business endeavours.

The heart of the plan is the Munich Airport Center (MAC) which will establish a dominant east–west axis linking the existing Terminal West with a future Terminal East. A second axis orders all the uses in the Neutral Zone and runs through the center of the Hotel Kempinski. In its final phase the MAC will link the airport to the local and long-distance train networks.

The Hotel Kempinski is the first building in the Neutral Zone. The plan organization of the hotel corresponds to the airport level system: pedestrians circulate at level 03, and the roads and drop-off occur above at level 04. The level 03 entrance lobby can be reached either

Continued

1 Site/landscaping plan
2 Concept sketches
3 Hotel Kempinski, covered walkways, and control tower
4 Aerial view
5 Landscaping

3

4

5

Hotel Kempinski/Munich Airport Center/Walkways   175

from the main terminal via the covered walkways, or from the below-grade parking structure in front of the hotel.

A glass stair and elevators lead to the main atrium at level 04. In concept, the atrium is both a private space for the hotel as well as a public reception hall for the expanding airport city. The transparency of the cable-supported glass end walls provides visual continuity between the drop-off, atrium and *biergarten* terrace extending to the south.

Covered moving walkways connect the existing terminal with the Hotel Kempinski, the MAC and bus terminal, and also the High Security Terminal along the eastern apron. In the east–west direction, the walkways extend the existing level 03 circulation routes of the terminal out into the open landscape, and in the north–south direction, they align with the longitudinal axis of the Neutral Zone centered on the atrium of the Kempinski Hotel.

Continued

6 South elevation
7 Entrance/car approach
8 West facade/restaurant/garden walk
9–11 Curtain wall/roof details
12 Elevation/section
13 Hotel landscaping
14 Sheltered entrance

Hotel Kempinski/Munich Airport Center/Walkways

The walls of the walkways consist of curved, punched steel plate that is 50 per cent open and visually transparent, yet still solid enough to block strong winds and driven rain. The underslung steel roof structure mirrors the crossing arches of the Hotel Kempinski and MAC roofs.

Flanking the walkways are linear gardens. Hedges, interspersed with pyramidal evergreens are arranged perpendicular to the walkway structure, heightening the sense of motion. Where the walkways cross one another or enter the terminal, groves of tightly spaced birches set in bright orange crushed brick create points of transition and orientation. At these "decision points" the punched steel walls are replaced by full-height glass panels, letting in more daylight and affording clear views into the birch groves and the landscape beyond.

15
16

15   Typical hotel room plan
16   Night view of atrium
17–18 Stair/glass wall
19   Geranium wall
20   Glass stair, lower level

17

18

19

20

Hotel Kempinski/Munich Airport Center/Walkways 179

21

22

21 Elevation/plan/section: cable wall
22 Glass end wall
23 Terrace garden
24 Entrance wall
25 Flower wall

Hotel Kempinski/Munich Airport Center/Walkways

26 Terrace
27 Glass flower wall
28 Stair, tree and flower wall
29 Glass flower wall dividers
30 Stair cores
31 Glass pattern wall
32 Tree detail
33 Flower wall detail

Hotel Kempinski/Munich Airport Center/Walkways   183

34

35

36

37

38

34 Stair
35 Cable wall connection
36 Walkway viewed from above
37 Fritted pattern glass
38 Stair
39 Underground walkway to garage
40 Walkway at night
41–42 Walkway connection to hotel

Hotel Kempinski/Munich Airport Center/Walkways

43

44

43 Munich Airport Center
44 Interior MAC pavilion
45 Concept sketches: MAC
46 Glass stair from walkway level to atrium
47–49 Walkway details

Hotel Kempinski/Munich Airport Center/Walkways

50 Walkway detail
51–52 Perforated metal detail
53 East–west walkway connection
54 Walkway connection to surface parking

53

54

Hotel Kempinski/Munich Airport Center/Walkways 189

Dearborn Station

Design/Completion 1994/1997
Dearborn, Michigan
Union Station Company
80,000 square feet
Lightweight steel cable trusses
Exterior membrane of Teflon-coated fiberglass alternating with clear vision glass

The new Amtrak station to be located in Dearborn, Michigan, will be a state-of-the-art transportation facility, specifically designed for the high-speed rail system that will ultimately link Detroit with Chicago, St Louis, Milwaukee, and beyond. The station will simultaneously serve as an exhibition space for Greenfield Village, an exhibition complex containing one of the world's largest collections of transportation technology.

The design of the 900-foot-long station is based on a cable-truss structural system which supports an enclosure of fabric and glass. The elliptical form totally envelopes the platform/exhibition space, as well as the passenger cars and locomotive of the high-speed train. Access to the elevated platform is via the Amtrak ticket station at the west end, and via the Greenfield Village entrance to the east.

1 Concept sketches
2 The 900-foot-long station
3 Station interior
4 Station exterior
5 Station interior

Dearborn Station 191

Bangkok International Airport

Design/Completion 1994/2001
Bangkok, Thailand
Airports Authority of Thailand
4,500,000 square feet
Steel frame with long-span trusses; concourses are three hinged, cable-stayed arches
Glass and metal panel curtain wall

The Second Bangkok International Airport will be a phased development located on a vacant site outside of Bangkok. Murphy/Jahn submitted three schemes in the competition.

Concept A
This concept emphasizes passenger circulation over aircraft circulation. Because the curbfront area is not capable of providing for the ultimate capacity of the site, two separate entrances were necessary; however, this is still the most compact terminal of those studied.

A large roof trellis structure placed over the complex of functionally separate buildings unifies the site and provides an overriding consistent architectural image. Sized to accommodate future growth, the trellis provides an important functional advantage as well as an architectural one.

Continued

1 Concept A: design sketch
2 Concept A: aerial view/plan
3 Concept A: roof trellis, ticketing area and tubular concourses
4 Concept A: roof trellis structure

Bangkok International Airport 193

Concept B-1
By increasing the aircraft maneuvering area between concourses, Concept B-1 balances airside circulation and passenger circulation. It can be expanded so that its curbfront can accommodate more than 60 million passengers without the need for a second airport entrance to a second terminal complex.

Its architecture is based on a unit structural module of triangular domed segments. Each segment has an outer roof shell, an inner airspace containing the structural members, and an inside ceiling surface. Triangular skylights are located on the outer surface.

Concept B-2
Because of its functional configuration, Concept B-2 provides the greatest airside efficiency of all the concepts studied. Like Concept B-1, this concept could be adapted to either a single or double-entrance master plan. It requires, however, an automated people-mover in the first phase.

5   Concept A: ticketing pavilion
6   Concept A: tubular concourse
7   Concept A: airside view
8–9 Concept B-1: triangular dome segments/courtyard
10–11 Concept B-2: double cantilevered folded plate truss

Bangkok International Airport   195

Flughafen Köln/Bonn Terminal 2

Design/Completion 1992/2000
Cologne, Germany
Flughafen Köln/Bonn GmbH
5,000,000 square feet
Steel roof and columns placed on concrete frame substructure
Aluminum and glass curtain wall

The existing airport is a landmark in the landscape. A reconfiguration is required to accommodate passenger growth and because new plane types require new functional and circulation areas as well as new security standards and updated baggage handling. The building program begins with the construction of the new terminal, Concourse D, Parking Structure North and the renovation of the existing terminal. This phase more than doubles the existing passenger volume by the year 2000.

The expansion extends the horizontal forms of the existing terminal, using lightweight steel rather than concrete. Similar to the existing terminal, the new buildings employ a repetitive long-span structure, establishing continuity in the scale and spirit of structural expression.

The construction consists of steel piers supporting a steel roof structure with diagonal skylights. This kind of repetitive "systems building" is ideal for phased construction, provides operational flexibility, and can be expanded in a very natural and rational sequence.

1 Design sketches
2 Landside/terminal/parking facility, phase II
3 Existing terminal with new terminal, phase I
4 Airside view, phase I

3

4

Flughafen Köln/Bonn Terminal 2 197

5

6

198

5   Covered drop-off
6   Meeters/greeters lobby
7   Bi-level roadway serving arrivals and departures
8   Ticketing/departure hall

Flughafen Köln/Bonn Terminal 2   199

Hyatt Regency Roissy

Design/Completion 1988/1992
Paris, France
Hyatt International Corporation; Toa Investment Pte. Ltd
Associate Architect: Arte J.M. Charpentier
280,000 square feet (400 rooms)
Concrete structure and steel roof structure
Painted aluminum panels and mullion system with fritted and clear vision glass on a tile base
Painted steel and fritted glass roof structure and end-walls

The Hyatt Regency is a 400-room airport hotel for short-term stays, facilitating travel in and out of the Charles de Gaulle Airport. It includes meeting facilities, bistro cafe, restaurant and health club facilities.

The design is a modern interpretation of the traditional Parisian courtyard hotel. The central axis of the project is defined by two five-story hotel room blocks which form the edges for the exterior courtyard garden and the interior atrium garden. The exterior garden is further defined by a curving garden trellis wall executed in steel and glass. This central axis is terminated by the conference facility which is situated between the two hotel wings.

Two double-loaded linear hotel room wings form the basis of the plan. The top three floors of these wings contain the required 400 rooms. The lower two floors contain the front-of-house and support spaces for the interior garden atrium, bistro cafe, lobby bar, and ballroom/meeting room facility.

1 Axonometric
2 Site plan
3 Two five-story hotel room blocks with central atrium
4 Outdoor landscaped court with windscreen

Hyatt Regency Roissy 201

5

6

7

5 Landscaped court
6 Entrance
7 Courtyard from arrival arcade
8 Courtyard at night
9 Atrium seating
10 Restaurant enclosure walls in atrium
11 Atrium interior

Hyatt Regency Roissy 203

King Abdulaziz International Airport Competition

Design 1991
Jeddah, Saudi Arabia
International Airport Projects, Ministry of Defense and Aviation
9,000,000 square feet
Steel frame with long-span trusses infilled with metal panel and tinted colored glass
Stainless steel and glass curtain wall

The competition for a new dual-terminal complex for the King Abdulaziz International Airport in Jeddah provided an opportunity to push airport design to yet further limits. Its size of 90 gates equals that of Chicago's O'Hare International Airport.

A simple arch spans the whole site, unifying the two buildings and creating a central space with mosque and gardens.

Functionally, the building is organized as a terminal concourse. Between the upper departure level and the lower arrival level, an intermediate pedestrian level is inserted, connecting the park and parking garage with the terminal buildings. The concourses have separate departure and arrival levels for international flights and also allow swing-use for domestic flights. Departing and arriving are carefully orchestrated sequences of varying spatial experiences which afford a continually varying sense of place and orientation. The passenger moves through the facility in a direct, logical way and can enjoy the experience.

1 Concept sketch
2 Site plan
3 90-gate terminal facility
4 Central pavilion
5 Departures/gate area

King Abdulaziz International Airport Competition 205

King Abdulaziz International Airport Conceptual Design

Design 1993
4,500,000 square feet
Modular steel-framed structural units
Stainless steel and glass curtain wall with lowered shading devices

Following the design competition, the site was changed. The objective was to provide a clear site allowing for the phased implementation of a new terminal without disruption to any existing operations.

The design concept selected uses domed segments as the elementary structural unit. Each segment acts together with the others surrounding it to form an efficient, highly sculptural roof system. The distinctive skylight pattern alternates from the outside surface of the roof to the inner surface. As a result, all natural light is filtered and indirect.

Landscaping is an integral part of the design. A large, stepped, central courtyard brings natural light and outside views to all levels of the building.

6 Departure and arrival plans
7 Ticketing pavilion with segmented domes
8 Airside elevation showing hold room curtain wall
9 Landside view

SECTION ELEVATION

PLAN

8

| 0 5 10 20ft |
| 0 1.5 3 6m |

9

King Abdulaziz International Airport 207

One America Plaza/Trolley Station

Design/Completion 1988/1991
San Diego, California
Shimizu Corporation
660,000 square feet
Steel perimeter columns, concrete core; exposed steel structure in station
Granite-clad columns with silicone-glazed unitized wall panels; horizontal stone spandrels with blue reflective glass infill at corners

This building is the key component in a mixed-use complex located in downtown San Diego, bordered by Broadway, Kettner, India, and B Streets. The 34-story tower fronts on Broadway, the main east–west artery of the central business district. Wrapping around the tower at plaza level is the San Diego trolley; the enclosed trolley station serves as the focal point of the two-story retail arcade which follows the serpentine form of the tracks.

The curving space of the trolley station also resolves the situation at the end of C Street, spatially linking this corridor to the plaza in front of the Santa Fe Depot. The result is an urban complex which animates the street with pedestrian activity, clarifies its relationship with the surrounding pattern of streets and open space, and incorporates a variety of public spaces.

1 Overall view from India and Broadway Streets
2 Ground-floor plan
3–5 Trolley station

3

4 5

One America Plaza/Trolley Station 209

JFK Consolidated Terminal

Design 1988
Jamaica, New York
American Airlines/Port Authority of NY/NJ
1,800,000 square feet
Steel frame with long-span, triangulated arched trusses with metal and glass infill
Steel and glass curtain wall

The terminal is configured as a four-level structure. The lower level contains all federal inspectional services areas, domestic claim areas, mechanical/electrical space and a large meeters/greeters lobby to serve the arriving passengers, their visitors and the deplaning curbfront. The grade level contains both inbound and outbound baggage systems, the PDS station and mechanical space, and ramp operations. The upper level contains ticketing, gate facilities, VIP lounges, and the enplaning curbfront. The penthouse level contains the FIS arrivals corridor and mechanical fan rooms.

The satellite concourse is configured as a three-level structure. The grade level contains ramp operations and mechanical/electrical rooms, the upper level contains gate facilities and concessions, and the penthouse level contains FIS arrival corridors and mechanical fan rooms.

1 Site plan
2 Concept sketch
3–4 Terminal with landside/airside concourse

JFK Consolidated Terminal 211

5   Section
6   End wall
7   Hold room with train connection to satellite facility
8–10 Ticketing pavilion

8

9

10

JFK Consolidated Terminal 213

United Airlines Terminal One Complex

Design/Completion 1983/1987
Chicago, Illinois (O'Hare International Airport)
United Airlines
1,185,000 square feet
Folded steel truss at pavilion, perforated steel arches at concourse
External aluminum tube mullion supports; combination of clear, clear fritted, and tinted glass at vertical walls; prefabricated silicone-glazed units at vaults

The Terminal One Complex for United Airlines at Chicago's O'Hare International Airport provides 48 gates, 12 commuter parking positions and 1,400,000 square feet of operating facilities.

The two primary components of the project, Concourses B and C, form two linear structures with a length of 1,600 feet. A gap of 815 feet between them allows for dual taxiing of wide-bodied aircraft. Concourse C contains 30 gates, and the remaining 18 are in Concourse B. A commuter airline operation is housed in a related wing adjacent to Concourse B.

The planning of the complex is based on the concept of parallel concourses, a departure from the Y-shaped concourses prevalent at O'Hare. The parallel configuration eliminates the "dead-ends" created in the Y-shaped form. This reduces aircraft waiting time on the apron, allows two-way taxiing which expedites aircraft movement to the gates, and makes the total perimeter of Concourse C available for aircraft parking.

1 Site plan
2 Landside Concourse B: departure drop-off
3 Sections
4 Concourse B: airside view
5 Overall view of Concourses B and C

TERMINAL 1 • CONCOURSE B

SATELLITE • CONCOURSE C

United Airlines Terminal One Complex

6

ROOF PLAN | LOWER LEVEL PLAN
UPPER LEVEL PLAN | BASEMENT PLAN

7

6 Concourse plans
7 Roadway
8 Curtain wall detail
9 Stair detail
10 Pedestrian tunnel access
11 Concourse B interior

United Airlines Terminal One Complex 217

12   Ticketing pavilion
13   Concourse B termination
14–15 Underground pedestrian tunnel
16   Concourse B vault

United Airlines Terminal One Complex 219

O'Hare Rapid Transit Station

Design/Completion 1979/1984
Chicago, Illinois
Chicago Building Commission
Reinforced post-tension concrete with sprayed concrete sloping berms
Glass block walls

The O'Hare Rapid Transit Extension is the final link between the Chicago Loop and Chicago O'Hare International Airport. The station, which becomes the terminus of the rapid transit line, is located beneath the O'Hare Parking Structure and consists of two components: the trainroom and the pedestrian concourse.

The trainroom contains three tracks and two platforms, and is approximately 600 feet long, 70 feet wide, and 30 feet high. The pedestrian concourse, which connects the station with four underground pedestrian tunnels leading to the three airport terminals and the hotel, is approximately 1,100 feet long, 45 feet wide and 18 feet high.

To obtain a column-free platform area, the structural system developed for the station consists of large post-tensioned concrete girders which transfer the load from the parking structure columns above the trainroom. This system will be constructed using an open-cut excavation, resulting in sloping berms sprayed with concrete outside the trainroom for the entire length of the station.

1 Site plan
2 Three-track platfrom
3 Ticketing area
4 Train platform
5 Train platform with glass block wall

O'Hare Rapid Transit Station

Firm Profile

Office of Murphy/Jahn, Architects

The office of Murphy/Jahn, Architects is located on one full and two partial floors. The design is based on classical principles of space organization for an architect's office: open design studios for free communication and collegial exchange of ideas, centrally located functional support systems, and formal "front offices" and conference/presentation rooms.

The central location of the building's core led to a tri-part configuration. Design studios are located to the east, west, and south of the core, with the reception area, conference rooms, and principals' offices logically placed on the north, just off the elevator banks.

The main corridor, executed in black terrazzo, encircles the core and clearly defines the main circulation. A stair, consisting of two tubular trusses painted red, is visible from the reception area and indicates the presence of Murphy/Jahn on another floor.

1 Circulation corridor
2 Computer area
3 Drafting area
4 Computer area

Cupola

The cupola is located on the fortieth floor of the building occupied by Murphy/Jahn, Architects. Its original use is unknown, but it had been divided into a myriad of small spaces for use by a law firm.

Murphy/Jahn remodeled the space for use as a client presentation/conference area. This involved completely stripping the structure and recreating the entity of the dome. Four service modules were created around two axes of symmetry, and the centrally located smokestack which had to be retained. The floor was raised 3 feet to allow for better views through the windows which had unusually high parapets.

The cupola is reached by an elaborate, round, 1920s elevator reminiscent of the French cage type, which has been authentically restored.

5 Cupola: presentation area, 3 story windows and bird cage elevator
6 Cupola: central stack for building

Office of Murphy/Jahn, Architects 223

Biography

Helmut Jahn FAIA

Helmut Jahn was born in 1940 in Nŭrnberg, Germany. He graduated from the Technische Hochschule, Munich in 1965 and the following year moved to the United States to undertake graduate studies at the Illinois Institute of Technology, with Myron Goldsmith and Fazlur Kahn.

From 1967 to 1973 he worked with C.F. Murphy Associates as assistant to Gene Summers, being made Executive Vice President and Director of Planning and Design in 1973. In 1981 he became a Principal in Murphy/Jahn: the following year he became President of the practice, and in 1983 he was also made Chief Executive Officer.

Today, Helmut Jahn has been called Chicago's premiere architect who has dramatically changed the face of Chicago. His buildings have had a "staggering" influence on world architecture according to John Zukowsky. His growing national and international reputation has led to commissions across the United States, Canada, Europe and the Far East. He is committed to design excellence and the improvement of the urban environment. His projects have been recognized globally for design innovation, vitality and integrity. From the numerous publications on his work, one understands the excitement his work has generated in the public eye as well as professional journals and press. Murphy/Jahn's buildings have received numerous design awards and have been represented in architectural exhibitions around the world.

His design is both rational and intuitive; it attempts to give each building its own philosophical and intellectual base and establishes an opportunity to exploit its particular elements to achieve a visual and communicative statement. The rational part deals with the realities of a problem. The intuitive aspect deals with the theoretical, intellectual aspects—a subconscious ability to sense the intrinsic structure of a problem and establish priorities for the elements of design that deal with space, form, light, color and materials and the way architecture communicates through symbol and meaning of architectural language.

In addition to his work for the practice, he has taught at the University of Illinois Chicago Campus, was the Elliot Noyes Professor of Architectural Design at Harvard University and the Davenport Visiting Professor of Architectural Design at Yale University, and Thesis Professor at Illinois Institute of Technology.

Associates & Collaborators

Sam Scaccia
Executive Vice President, Director of Production
Sony Center, Berlin, Germany;
Principal Mutual Life Insurance Company, Des Moines, Iowa;
Charlemagne, Brussels, Belgium;
Victoria Berlin, Berlin, Germany;
Munich Airport Center, Munich, Germany;
Stralauer Platz 35, Berlin, Germany;
Kempinski Hotel, Munich, Germany;
21 Century Tower, Shanghai, China;
Ku-Damm 70, Berlin, Germany;
Pallas, Stuttgart, Germany;
United Airlines Terminal One Complex, Chicago, Illinois;
Messeturm, Frankfurt, Germany;
Northwestern Atrium Center, Chicago, Illinois;
425 Lexington Avenue, New York, New York;
One Liberty Place, Philadelphia, Pennsylvania;
120 North LaSalle, Chicago, Illinois;
Park Avenue Tower, New York, New York;
750 Lexington Avenue, New York, New York;
Cityspire, New York, New York;
Barnett Center, Jacksonville, Florida;
O'Hare Development Program, Chicago, Illinois;
Hyatt Regency Roissy, Paris, France;
Credit Lyonnais Bank Nederland, Rotterdam, The Netherlands;
300 East 85th Street, New York, New York

Philip Castillo
Senior Vice President, Principal Architect
21 Century Tower, Shanghai, China;
Sony Center Berlin, Germany;
Credit Lyonnais Bank Nederland, Rotterdam, The Netherlands;
Fort Canning Tower, Singapore;
Kongresshotel Messe, Frankfurt, Germany;
Tokyu-Shibuya Tower, Tokyo, Japan;
Kuala Lumpur City Center 2, Kuala Lumpur, Malaysia;
Lego Tower;
Wan-Chai Competition, Hong Kong;
Caltex Tower, Singapore;
Hitachi Tower, Singapore;
Celebration Center, Orlando, Florida;
Navy Pier, Chicago, Illinois;
MM21 Project, Yokohama, Japan;
Tokyo Teleport Town, Tokyo, Japan;
World's Tallest Building;
Dockland Square, London, England;
North Loop Block 37, Chicago, Illinois;
Citizens and Southern Bank, Atlanta, Georgia;
Wells & Lake Office Tower, Chicago, Illinois;
Niebelungenplatz, Frankfurt, Germany;
Oakbrook Terrace Tower, Oakbrook, Illinois;
362 West Street, Durban, South Africa;
Parktown Stands 85/87 and 102/103, Johannesburg, South Africa;
Merchandise Mart Bridge, Chicago, Illinois;
One South Wacker, Chicago, Illinois;
Madison Square Garden "Penn Gate", New York, New York

Brian J. O'Connor
Senior Vice President, Principal Architect
United Airlines Terminal One Complex, Chicago, Illinois;
O'Hare Development Program, Chicago, Illinois;
Flughafen Köln/Bonn, Cologne, Germany;
King Abdulaziz International Airport, Jeddah, Saudi Arabia;
Consolidated Terminal Project, JFK International Airport, Jamaica, New York;
American Airlines Terminal, JFK International Airport, Jamaica, New York;
Bangkok International Airport Competition, Bangkok, Thailand;
Okinawa Airport Competition, Okinawa, Japan;
Logan Airport Competition, Boston, Massachusetts;
Harold Washington Library Center Competition, Chicago, Illinois

Rainer Schildknecht
Senior Vice President, Principal Architect
Victoria Berlin, Berlin, Germany;
Stralauer Platz 35, Berlin, Germany;
Munich Airport Center, Munich, Germany;
Europa-Haus, Frankfurt, Germany;
Ku-Damm 119, Berlin, Germany;
Kempinski Hotel/Garage, Flughafen München 2, Munich, Germany;
Master Plan Neutral Zone, Flughafen München 2, Munich, Germany;
Ku-Damm 70, Berlin, Germany;
Munich Order Center, Munich, Germany;
Pallas, Stuttgart, Germany;
Mannheimer Lebensversicherung, Mannheim, Germany;
Messeturm, Frankfurt, Germany;
Messehalle, Frankfurt, Germany;
Northwestern Atrium Center, Chicago, Illinois;
Chicago Board of Trade Addition, Chicago, Illinois;
Area 2 Police Headquarters, Chicago, Illinois

Martin F. Wolf
Senior Vice President, Principal Architect
Flughafen Köln/Bonn, Cologne, Germany;
Principal Mutual Life Insurance Company, Des Moines, Iowa;
King Abdulaziz International Airport, Jeddah, Saudi Arabia;
Amtrak Station, Dearborn, Michigan;
Reichstagsgebäude Competition, Berlin, Germany;
Berlin 2000 Sports Complex, Berlin, Germany;
Bangkok International Airport Competition, Bangkok, Thailand;
American Airlines Terminal Complex, JFK International Airport, Jamaica, New York;
One America Plaza, San Diego, California;
Munich Airport Center, Munich, Germany;
First & Broadway, Los Angeles Civic Center, Los Angeles, California;
9th & Figueroa, Los Angeles, California;
Television City, New York, New York;
United Airlines Terminal One Complex, Chicago, Illinois;
Northwestern Atrium Center, Chicago, Illinois;
Bank of the Southwest Tower, Houston, Texas;
Naiman Sports Club, Chicago, Illinois;
Federal Life Insurance Company, Deerfield, Illinois;
O'Hare Development Program, Chicago, Illinois;
Monarch Beach Office Building, Dana Point, California;
Fountain Square West, Cincinnati, Ohio;
Chicago Board of Trade Addition, Chicago, Illinois;
FIS International Terminal Four, Chicago, Illinois;
Automated Guideway Transit Stations, Chicago, Illinois;
Security Bay Expansion, Chicago, Illinois;
Chicago Sports Complex, Chicago, Illinois

Associates & Collaborators Continued

Gordon Beckman
Vice President, Senior Project Architect
Jakarta Communications Tower, Jakarta, Indonesia;
Victoria Berlin, Berlin, Germany;
Charlemagne, Brussels, Belgium;
Hamburg, Altona, Germany;
QCD, Mexico City, Mexico;
Salzufer, Berlin, Germany;
Alexanderplatz, Berlin, Germany;
Kaufhof Turm, Berlin, Germany;
MM21 Project, Yokohama, Japan;
Augustinerhof, Nuernberg, Germany;
CBC Tower, Toronto, Canada;
Place de Ville, Ottawa, Canada;
Wells and Lake Office Tower, Chicago, Illinois;
Hyatt Regency Roissy, Paris, France;
Amsterdam Master Plan, Amsterdam, The Netherlands;
Credit Lyonnais Bank Nederland, Rotterdam, The Netherlands;
TSP Competition Essen, Essen, Germany;
Kuala Lumpur City Center 2, Kuala Lumpur, Malaysia;
Barnett Center, Jacksonville, Florida;
Lake and Wells Office Tower, Chicago, Illinois;
750 Lexington Avenue, New York, New York;
Pacific Basin Tower, California;
Metro West, Naperville, Illinois

Steven S. Cook
Vice President, Senior Project Architect
Flughafen Köln/Bonn, Cologne, Germany;
Columbus Pier, St Pauli, Hamburg, Germany;
Munich Airport Center, Munich, Germany;
MUC 2 Walkways, Munich, Germany;
Munich Order Center, Munich, Germany;
Infrastruktur Flughafen München 2, Munich, Germany;
Kempinski Hotel and Parking Garage, Germany;
Pallas, Stuttgart, Germany;
Ku-Damm 70, Berlin, Germany;
1111 Brickell Avenue, Miami, Florida;
Mannheimer Lebensversicherung, Mannheim, Germany;
Mannheim-Ost: Tec Platz, Mannheim, Germany;
Ku-Damm 119, Berlin, Germany;
Messeturm, Frankfurt, Germany;
Madison Square Garden "Penn Gate", New York, New York;
First & Broadway, Los Angeles Civic Center, Los Angeles, California;
Park Avenue Tower, New York, New York

John S. Durbrow
Vice President, Senior Project Architect
Endless Towers, Singapore;
Jakarta Tower Kuningan Centre, Indonesia
Gehrlinghaus, Köln, Germany;
Mehringplatz, Berlin, Germany;
120 North LaSalle, Chicago, Illinois;
Europa-Haus, Frankfurt Germany;
Harold Washington Library Center Competition, Chicago, Illinois;
Victoria Berlin, Berlin, Germany;
Victoria Versicherung Competition, Düsseldorf, Germany;
Stuttgart/Berliner Platz, Stuttgart, Germany;
Hamburg Station Project, Hamburg, Germany;
Place de Ville III, Ottawa, Canada;
P&C/FWW Department Store, Berlin, Germany;
Hessische Landesbank Competition, Frankfurt, Germany;
Lufthansa Headquarters, Cologne, Germany;
Alliance Airport Terminal—Administration Building, Fort Worth, Texas;
Monmouth County Office Building, Monmouth, New Jersey;
Stralauer Platz 35, Berlin, Germany;
IHZ Tower, Düsseldorf, Germany;
Landesgirokasse Bank Center, Stuttgart, Germany;
Alexanderplatz, Berlin, Germany

Susan Froelich
Vice President, Senior Project Architect
21 Century Tower, Shanghai, China;
Sony Center Berlin, Germany;
Flughafen Köln/Bonn, Cologne, Germany;
King Abdulaziz International Airport, Jeddah, Saudi Arabia;
Tokyo Teleport Town, Tokyo, Japan;
Munich Airport Center, Munich, Germany;
Madison Square Garden "Penn Gate", New York, New York;
One America Plaza, San Diego California;
Ku-Damm 119, Berlin, Germany;
Messe Riem Urban Competition, Munich, Germany;
Monmouth County Office Building, Monmouth, New Jersey;
Northwestern Atrium Center West, Chicago, Illinois;
First & Broadway, Los Angeles Civic Center, Los Angeles, California;
Fort Canning Tower, Singapore;
North Loop Block 37, Chicago, Illinois;
Livingston Plaza, Brooklyn, New York;
Two Liberty Place, Philadelphia, Pennsylvania

Scott Pratt
Senior Vice President, Senior Project Architect
Sony Center Berlin, Germany;
Hyatt Regency Roissy, Paris, France;
One Liberty Place, Philadelphia, Pennsylvania;
Two Liberty Place, Philadelphia, Pennsylvania;
Wilshire/Westwood, Los Angeles, California;
9th & Figueroa, Los Angeles, California;
1000 West Sixth Street, Los Angeles, California;
Park Place, Los Angeles, California;
West Loop Office Project, Chicago, Illinois;
Houston Tower, Houston, Texas;
Northbrook Centre, Northbrook, Illinois;
West Loop Pedway, Chicago, Illinois;
701 Fourth Avenue South, Minneapolis, Minnesota;
One Hennepin Center, Minneapolis, Minnesota;
The Esplanade, Houston, Texas;
Hyatt Regency Frankfurt am Main, Frankfurt, Germany;
University of Illinois Agricultural Engineering Sciences Building, Urbana-Champaign, Illinois;
First Source Center, South Bend, Indiana;
W.W. Grainger Corporate Headquarters, Skokie, Illinois;
Oakbrook Post Office, Oakbrook, Illinois

Dennis Recek (1968–1990)
Vice President, Senior Project Architect
120 North LaSalle, Chicago, Illinois;
One America Plaza, San Diego, California;
Wilshire/Westwood, Los Angeles, California;
1000 West Sixth Street, Los Angeles, California;

Harold Washington Library Center
Competition, Chicago, Illinois;
Metro West, Naperville, Illinois

Dieter Zabel
Vice President, Senior Project Architect
Mehringplatz, Berlin, Germany;
Stralauer Platz 35, Berlin, Germany;
Sony Center Berlin, Germany;
Grossmarkthalle, Frankfurt, Germany;
Reichstagsgebäude Competition, Berlin, Germany;
Berlin 2000 Sports Complex, Berlin, Germany;
Regierungsviertel Spreebogen Competition, Berlin, Germany;
Urban Competition Alexanderplatz, Berlin, Germany;
Europa-Haus, Frankfurt, Germany;
Ku-Damm 119, Berlin, Germany;
Kongresshotel Messe, Frankfurt, Germany;
Messe Riem Urban Competition, Munich, Germany;
Munich Airport Center Infrastruktur, Munich, Germany;
P&C/FWW Department Store, Berlin, Germany;
Victoria Versicherung Competition, Düsseldorf, Germany;
Helaba, Frankfurt, Germany;
Messeturm, Frankfurt, Germany;
Messehalle, Frankfurt, Germany;
Mannheimer Lebensversicherung, Mannheim, Germany

Edward P. Wilkas
Vice President, Director of Production
Principal Mutual Life Insurance Company, Des Moines, Iowa;
120 North LaSalle, Chicago, Illinois;
Hyatt Regency Roissy, Paris, France;
North Loop Block 37, Chicago, Illinois;
GSA Office Building Competition, Chicago, Illinois;
West Loop Pedway, Chicago, Illinois;
One Liberty Place, Philadelphia, Pennsylvania;
State of Illinois Center, Chicago, Illinois;
Randolph Street Pedway, Chicago, Illinois;
Lake/Clark Transfer Station, Chicago, Illinois

Mark Joshua Frisch
Director of Production
Victoria Berlin, Berlin, Germany;
Europa-Haus, Frankfurt, Germany;
Ku-Damm 119, Berlin, Germany;
Munich Order Center, Munich, Germany;
Hyatt Regency Roissy, Paris, France;
Messeturm, Frankfurt, Germany;
Messehalle, Frankfurt, Germany;
Two Liberty Place, Philadelphia Pennsylvania;
One Liberty Place Competition, Philadelphia, Pennsylvania;
Cityspire, New York, New York;
Park Avenue Tower, New York, New York;
O'Hare Development Program, Chicago, Illinois

Sanford E. Gorshow
Director of Production
Stralauer Platz 35, Berlin, Germany;
Principal Mutual Life Insurance Company, Des Moines, Iowa;
Europa-Haus, Frankfurt, Germany;
Munich Order Center, Munich, Germany;
Monarch Beach Office Building, Dana Point, California;
Pallas, Stuttgart, Germany;
Ku-Damm 70, Berlin, Germany;
Mannheimer Lebensversicherung, Mannheim, Germany;
United Airlines Terminal One Complex, Chicago, Illinois;
Shand Morahan, Evanston, Illinois;
Plaza East, Milwaukee, Wisconsin

Stephen Kern
Director of Production
21 Century Tower, Shanghai, China;
Sony Center Berlin, Berlin, Germany;
Credit Lyonnais Bank Nederland, Rotterdam, The Netherlands;
Hyatt Regency Roissy, Paris, France;
Messeturm, Frankfurt, Germany;
Messehalle, Frankfurt, Germany;
Merchandise Mart Bridge, Chicago, Illinois;
One Liberty Place, Philadelphia, Pennsylvania;
425 Lexington Avenue, New York, New York;
362 West Street, Durban, South Africa;
Northwestern Atrium Center, Chicago, Illinois

Steven Michael Nilles
Director of Production
Sony Center, Berlin, Germany;
Munich Airport Center, Munich, Germany;
Kempinski Hotel, Munich, Germany;
MUC 2 Tiefgarage, Munich, Germany;
Livingston Plaza, Brooklyn, New York;
Barnett Center, Jacksonville, Florida;
Northern Trust Pedestrian Bridge, Chicago, Illinois;
Messehalle, Frankfurt, Germany;
Wilshire/Westwood, Los Angeles, California;
United Airlines Terminal One Complex, Chicago, Illinois

Thomas M. Chambers
Project Architect
Flughafen Köln/Bonn, Cologne, Germany;
Midway Terminal Improvement Program, Chicago, Illinois;
Bangkok International Airport Competition, Bangkok, Thailand;
United Airlines Terminal One Complex, Chicago, Illinois;
King Abdulaziz International Airport, Jeddah, Saudi Arabia;
American Airlines Terminal Complex, JFK International Airport, Jamaica, New York;
O'Hare Development Program, Chicago, Illinois;
Consolidated Terminal Project, JFK International Airport, Jamaica, New York;
Mannheimer Lebensversicherung, Mannheim, Germany;
Monarch Beach Office Building, Dana Point, California;
Harold Washington Library Center Competition, Chicago, Illinois;
Park Place Competition, Los Angeles, California;
Italian Sports Complex, Rome, Italy

Consulting Architects
Charles Bostick
Fritz Ludwig
Lothar Pascher
Raimund Schock

Former Senior Personnel
Daniel Dolan
James Goettsch
Robert Goldberg
James M. Stevenson

Chronological List of Buildings & Projects
(By year of project commencement)

*Indicates work featured in this book
 (see Selected and Current Works).

Mat-Buildings

H. Roe Bartle Exhibition Hall
Kansas City, Missouri
Design 1972/Completion 1976
C.F. Murphy Associates
In joint venture with:
 Seligson Associates
 Hormer and Blessing
 Howard Needles Tammen Bergendoff

*Kemper Arena
Kansas City, Missouri
Design 1973/Completion 1974
American Royal Arena Corporation

John Marshall Courts Building
Richmond, Virginia
Design 1973/Completion 1976
Richmond Court Facility

Fourth District Courts Building
Maywood, Illinois
Design 1974/Completion 1976
Cook County Building Commission

*Auraria Library
Denver, Colorado
Design 1974/Completion 1976
Auraria Higher Education District

*Michigan City Public Library
Michigan City, Indiana
Design 1974/Completion 1977
Michigan City Public Library System

*Saint Mary's Athletic Facility
South Bend, Indiana
Design 1976/Completion 1977
Saint Mary's College

*Rust-Oleum Corporation Headquarters
Vernon Hills, Illinois
Design 1976/Completion 1979
Rust-Oleum Corporation

Commonwealth Edison District Headquarters
Bolingbrook, Illinois
Design 1976/Completion 1979
Commonwealth Edison

*De La Garza Career Center
East Chicago, Indiana
Design 1976/Completion 1981
City of East Chicago

*Minnesota Government & History Center
St Paul, Minnesota
Design 1976
State of Minnesota

Mat-Buildings continued

*Abu Dhabi Conference Center City
United Emirates
Design 1976
United Arab Emirates

La Lumiere Gymnasium
La Porte, Indiana
Design 1977/Completion 1978
La Lumiere School

Oakbrook Post Office
Oakbrook, Illinois
Design 1978/Completion 1981
United States Post Office

*Area 2 Police Headquarters
Chicago, Illinois
Design 1978/Completion 1981
City of Chicago

*ANL/DOE Program Support Facility
Argonne, Illinois
Design 1978/Completion 1981
US Department of Energy

**University of Illinois
Ag. Eng. Science Building**
Urbana-Champaign, Illinois
Design 1978/Completion 1984
State of Illinois, Capital Development Board

COD/Learning Resources Center
Glen Ellyn, Illinois
Design 1979/Completion 1983
State of Illinois, Capital Development Board

***Wisconsin Residence**
Eagle River, Wisconsin
Design 1980/Completion 1982
Private residence

Codex Corporate Headquarters
Canton, Massachusetts
Design 1982
Codex Corporation

Exposition and Office Complex
Chicago, Illinois
Design 1982

Parktown Stands
Johannesburg, South Africa
Design 1984/Completion 1986
Anglo American Properties
Associate Architect:
    John Kemp & Associates

*San Diego Convention Center
San Diego, California
Design 1984
San Diego Convention Bureau
In joint venture with:
    Martinez/Wong Associates, Inc.

Chronological List of Buildings & Projects   231

Mat-Buildings continued

Messe Hall 1
Design 1985/Completion 1988
Messe Hall Messe Frankfurt GmbH

Palace Prince Khaled
Saudi Arabia
Design 1987
Private Residence

*Munich Order Center
Munich, Germany
Design 1989/Completion 1993
Archimedes Gewerbe - und Buero Centrum GmbH & Co.

Monarch Beach Office Building
Dana Point, California
Design 1989
Stein Brief Partnership

*Navy Pier
Chicago, Illinois
Design 1991
Metropolitan Pier and Exhibition Authority

*Celebration Center
Florida
Design 1991
Disney Development Co.

Messe Riem Urban Competition
Munich, Germany
Design 1992

Tower Buildings

*Xerox Centre
Chicago, Illinois
Design 1978/Completion 1980
Romanek-Golub

*Chicago Board of Trade Addition
Chicago, Illinois
Design 1978/Completion 1982
Chicago Board of Trade
In joint venture with:
    Shaw and Associates
    Swanke Hayden Connell Architects

*One South Wacker
Chicago, Illinois
Design 1979/Completion 1982
Metropolitan Structures/
    Harvey Walken & Co.

Plaza East
Milwaukee, Wisconsin
Design 1980/Completion 1982 (1)
Design 1981/Completion 1984 (2)
JMB Reality

*11 Diagonal Street
Johannesburg, South Africa
Design 1981/Completion 1984
Anglo American Properties
Associate Architect:
    Louis Karol Architects

701 Fourth Avenue South
Minneapolis, Minnesota
Design 1982/Completion 1984
Turner Development Corporation

Chronological List of Buildings & Projects

Tower Buildings continued

*Park Avenue Tower
New York, New York
Design 1982/Completion 1986
Park Tower Realty

*362 West Street
Durban, South Africa
Design 1983/Completion 1986
Anglo-American Properties
Associate Architect:
　　Stauch Vorster + Partners

*Metro West
Naperville, Illinois
Design 1984/Completion 1986
Westminister Corporation

*Northwestern Atrium Center
Chicago, Illinois
Design 1984/Completion 1987
Tishman Midwest Management Corp

*One Liberty Place
Philadelphia, Pennsylvania
Design 1984/Completion 1987
Rouse Associates

*Wilshire/Westwood
Los Angeles, California
Design 1984/Completion 1988
Developer: Platt Corporation
Owner: The Prospect Co.

*Cityspire
New York, New York
Design 1984/Completion 1989
West 56th Street Associates

*750 Lexington Avenue
New York, New York
Design 1984/Completion 1989
Cohen Brothers

*Oakbrook Terrace Tower
Oakbrook Terrace, Illinois
Design 1985/Completion 1987
Miglin Beitler Incorporated

300 East 85th Street
New York, New York
Design 1985/Completion 1988
East 85th Street Associates

*425 Lexington Avenue
New York, New York
Design 1985/Completion 1989
Olympia & York Equity Corporation

*Messe Tower/Messe Hall
Frankfurt, Germany
Design 1985/Completion 1991
TishmanSpeyer Properties of Germany, L.P.

Chronological List of Buildings & Projects

Tower Buildings continued

***Bank of Southwest Tower**
Houston, Texas
Design 1985
Century Development Corporation
Associate Architect:
 Lloyd Jones Brewer Associates

Pacific Basin Tower
Design 1985

Television City
New York, New York
Design 1985
Trump Organization

9th & Figueroa
Los Angeles, California
Design 1985
RCI

***Columbus Circle**
New York, New York
Design 1985
Trump Organization

***South Ferry Plaza**
New York, New York
Design 1986
Olympia & York Equity Corporation

Stuttgart/Berliner Platz
Stuttgart, Germany
Design 1986
OPUS Entwicklungsgesellschaft

1000 West Sixth Street
Los Angeles, California
Design 1987
Platt Corporation

*Barnett Center
Jacksonville, Florida
Design 1988/Completion 1990
Developer: Paragon Group, Inc.
Owner: Barnett Bank

*120 North LaSalle
Chicago, Illinois
Design 1988/Completion 1991
Ahmanson Commercial
　　Development Corporation

Two Liberty Place
Philadelphia, Pennsylvania
Design 1988/Completion 1991
Rouse Associates
Office Design Architect: Murphy/Jahn
Architect: Zeidler Roberts Partnership

One America Plaza
San Diego, California
Design 1988/Completion 1993
Shimizu Corporation

Tower Buildings continued

*Hitachi Tower
Singapore
Design 1988/Completion 1993
Savu Properties Pte.
Associate Architect: Architects 61

*Caltex House
Singapore
Design 1989/Completion 1993
Savu Properties Pte.
Associate Architect: Architects 61

Credit Lyonnais Bank Nederland
Rotterdam, The Netherlands
Design 1988/Completion 1995
Credit Lyonnais Bank Nederland
Associate Architect: Inbo Architektenburo

*The North Loop Block 37
Chicago, Illinois
Design 1988
FJV Venture

*1111 Brickell Avenue
Miami, Florida
Design 1988
1111 Brickell Associates

*Project J (1, 2, 3)
Chicago, Illinois
Design 1989
Howard Ecker & Co.

Wan-Chai Competition
Hong Kong
Design 1989
Sun Hung Kai Properties

Citizens & Southern Bank
Atlanta, Georgia
Design 1989
Citizens & Southern Bank

Canadian Broadcast Tower
Toronto, Canada
Design 1989

*Tokyo Teleport Town
Tokyo, Japan
Design 1990
Associate Architect: Kajima Corporation

World's Tallest Building
Design 1990

Dockland Square
London, England
Design 1990
Olympia & York

Chronological List of Buildings & Projects 239

Tower Buildings continued

*Yokohama Waterfront MM21 Project
Yokohama, Japan
Design 1990
Mitsui & Co.
Associate Architect:
    A.A.S. Associates Intíl. Co.

*Kuala Lumpur City Center 1
Kuala Lumpur, Malaysia
Design 1991
Seri Kuda Sdn. Bhd.

*FAA O'Hare Control Tower
Chicago, Illinois
Design 1991
Chicago O'Hare International Airport
Dept. of Aviation, City of Chicago

*Fountain Square West
Cincinnati, Ohio
Design 1991
The Galbreath Company

*IHZ Tower
Düsseldorf, Germany
Competition 1992
Premier GmbH Bouygues

*Fort Canning Tower
Singapore
Design 1992
Singapore Telecom
Associate Architect: Architects 61

*Tokyu-Shibuya Tower
Tokyo, Japan
Design 1992
Tokyu Corporation
Associate Architects:
    Kume Sekkei Co, Ltd
    Media Five

*21 Century Tower
Shanghai, China
Design 1993
Completion 1997
China Everbright International Trust
    and Investment Corp.
Associate Architect:
    East China Architectural Design Institute

*Jakarta Tower Kuningan Centre
Jakarta, Indonesia
Design 1994
Pacific Metrorealty

*Endless Towers
Singapore
Design 1995
Pidemco Land Limited
Associate Architect: Architects 61

*Jakarta Communications Tower
Jakarta, Indonesia
Design 1995
PT Kuningan Persada

Chronological List of Buildings & Projects   241

Urban Block Buildings

*First Source Center
South Bend, Indiana
Design 1978/Completion 1982
First Source Bank
Rahn Properties
City of South Bend

*State of Illinois Center
Chicago, Illinois
Design 1979/Completion 1985
State of Illinois, Capital Development Board
In joint venture with:
    Lester B. Knight & Associates

*Shand Morahan Corporate Headquarters
Evanston, Illinois
Design 1982/Completion 1984
Walken Souyoul Interests

Hague Town Hall and Library
Amsterdam, The Netherlands
1986

*First & Broadway Los Angeles Civic Center
Los Angeles, California
Design 1987
RCI

Livingston Plaza
Brooklyn, New York
Design 1988/Completion 1991
Developer: Cohen Brothers Realty
Client: NYCT

*Mannheimer Lebensversicherung Headquarters
Mannheim, Germany
Design 1988/Completion 1992
Mannheimer Lebensversicherung AG
Mannheimer Versicherung AG

*Ku-Damm 70
Berlin, Germany
Design 1988/Completion 1994
Euwo Unternehmensgruppe

*Ku-Damm 119
Berlin, Germany
Design 1988/Completion 1995
Athena Grundstuecks AG
Vebau GmbH Frankfurt/Berlin

*Harold Washington Library Center
Competition
Chicago, Illinois
Design 1988
City of Chicago Library System,
    Tishman Midwest

*Victoria Düsseldorf Competition
Düsseldorf, Germany
Design 1988
Victoria Versicherungsgesellschaft

*Pallas Office Building
Stuttgart, Germany
Design 1989/Completion 1994
IGEPA - Industrie - und
    Gewerbepark Bautraeger

Urban Block Buildings continued

***Augustinerhof-Nuernberg**
Nuernberg, Germany
Design 1990/Competion 1997
Abousaidy

***Lufthansa Corporate Headquarters**
Cologne, Germany
Design 1990
Lufthansa German

***Victoria Versicherungsgesellschaft**
Berlin, Germany
Design 1992/Completion 1997
Victoria Versicherungsgesellschaft

***Europa-Haus**
Frankfurt, Germany
Design 1992
SkanInvest

Landesgirokasse Bank Center Competition
Stuttgart, Germany
Design 1992
Landesgirokasse Bank

Communication Center FFM
Frankfurt, Germany
Design 1992

*Principal Mutual Life
Insurance Company
Des Moines, Iowa
Design 1993/Completion 1995
Principal Mutual Life Insurance Company

*Stralauer Platz 35
Berlin, Germany
Design 1993/Completion 1997
OPUS Entwicklungsgesellschaft

Columbus Pier
Hamburg, Germany
Design 1993/Completion 1997
Garbe Projekt-Entwicklung

*Sony Center, Berlin
Berlin, Germany
Design 1993/Completion 1998
Sony Corporation

Reichstagsgebaude Competition
Berlin, Germany
Design 1993

*Charlemagne
Brussels, Belgium
Design 1994
Etudes et Investissements
    Immobiliers, S.A./N.V.
Associate Architect: ARC, S.A. Architectes

Transportation Buildings

*O'Hare Rapid Transit Station
Chicago, Illinois
Design 1979/Completion 1984
Chicago Building Commission

*United Airlines Terminal One Complex
Chicago-O'Hare International Airport
Design 1983/Completion 1987
United Airlines

Merchandise Mart Bridge
Chicago, Illinois
Design 1987/Completion 1988
Merchandise Mart Properties

Alliance Airport Terminal, Administration Building
Fort Worth, Texas
Design 1988
Alliance Airport

West Loop Pedway
Chicago, Illinois
Design 1989
City of Chicago

*One America Plaza/Trolley Station
San Diego, California
Design 1988/Completion 1991
Shimizu Corporation

*Hyatt Regency Roissy
Paris, France
Design 1988/Completion 1992
Hyatt International Corporation
Toa Investment Pte., Ltd

*JFK Consolidated Terminal
Schematic Design
Jamaica, New York
Design 1988
American Airlines/Port Authority of NY/NJ

*Hotel Kempinski/Munich Airport Center /Walkways
Munich, Germany
Hotel Design 1989/Completion 1994
MAC Design 1990/Completion 1997
Walkways Design 1991/Completion 1992
Hotel/Walkways: Flughafen Munchen GmbH
MAC: Flughafen Munchen GmbH
    MFG Beta KG
    ALBA GmbH

Chronological List of Buildings & Projects 247

Transportation Buildings continued

*King Abdulaziz International Airport Competition, Conceptual Design, Schemes 1 & 2
Jeddah, Saudi, Arabia
Design 1991/1993
International Airport Projects
Ministry of Defense and Aviation

*Flughafen Köln/Bonn Terminal 1
Cologne, Germany
Design 1992/Completion 2000
Flughafen Köln/Bonn GmbH

*Dearborn Station
Dearborn, Michigan
Design 1994
Union Station Company

*Bangkok International Airport
Bangkok, Thailand
Design 1994/Completion 2001
Airports Authority of Thailand

Awards & Exhibitions

Awards

AIA Chicago Chapter Award
Hyatt Regency Roissy
1994

AIA Chicago Chapter Award
Munich Order Center
1994

Outstanding Achievement/Architect
Illinois Academy Of Fine Arts
1993

New Chicago Architecture Award
120 North LaSalle
1993

New Chicago Architecture Award
Sony/Berlin
1993

CIDB Best Buildable Design Awards
Hitachi Tower
1993

Bund Deutscher Architektan
Mannheimer Lebensversicherung
1993

IIT Award
For Outstanding Contribution to the Built Environment
1992

Chicago Architecture Award
American Institute Of Architects, Illinois Chapter/Merchandise Mart
1992

AIA San Diego Chapter Award
One America Plaza Trolley Station
1992

AIA Chicago Chapter Award
120 North LaSalle
1992

AIA Chicago Chapter Award
Mannheimer Lebensversicherung
1992

Ten Most Influential Living American Architects
American Institute of Architects
Helmut Jahn
1991

Ten Best Works of American Architecture Completed Since 1980
American Institute of Architects
State Of Illinois Center
1991

Ten Best Works of American Architecture Completed Since 1980
American Institute of Architects
United Airlines Terminal
1991

Development of the Year
Chicago Sun Times Real Estate
120 North LaSalle
1991

Dean of Architecture Award
Chicago Design Awards
1991

AIA Chicago Chapter Award
Messe Halle
1991

AIA Chicago Chapter Award
Wilshire/Westwood
1991

"Top 100 Architects"
Architectural Digest
1991

"The Top Ten" Chicago's Ten Most Important Post World War II Works of Architecture
State Of Illinois Center
Paul Gapp
1991

Quaternario International Award for Innovative Technology in Architecture
United Airlines Terminal
1990

Domino's 30 Award
1990

AISC Award
United Airlines Terminal
1990

AISC Award
One Liberty Place
1990

Divine Detail Honor Award
American Institute of Architects, Chicago Chapter
United Airlines Terminal
1990

AIA Chicago Chapter Award
One Liberty Place
1990

Domino's 30 Award
1989

American Consulting Engineers Council Award
United Airlines Terminal
1989

R.S. Reynolds Memorial Award
Annual Award for Distinguished Architecture Using Aluminum
United Airlines Terminal
1988

NEA Presidential Design Award
O'Hare Rapid Transit Station
1988

Chevalier Dans L'Ordre des Arts et des Lettres
Ministere de la Culture et de la Communication
Paris, France
Helmut Jahn
1988

Annual Design Review "Best of Category"
Industrial Design Magazine
United Airlines Terminal
1988

Twenty-Five Year Award
American Institute of Architects, Chicago Chapter
O'Hare International Airport
1988

AIA Chicago Chapter Award
United Airlines Terminal
1988

Structural Engineering Association of Illinois Award
United Airlines Terminal
1987

Annual Award
Concrete Industry Board of New York
Cityspire
1987

AIA National Honor Award
O'Hare Rapid Transit Station
1987

AIA National Honor Award
United Airlines Terminal
1987

AIA Chicago Chapter Award
Metro West
1987

Structural Engineering Association of Illinois Award
Northwestern Atrium Center
1986

AIA New York State Award
701 Fourth Avenue South
1986

AIA Chicago Chapter Award
State Of Illinois Center
1986

Structural Engineering Association of Illinois Award
Addition to the Chicago Board of Trade
1985

Structural Engineering Association of Illinois Award
State Of Illinois Center
1985

Progressive Architecture Award
Chicago Central Area Plan
1985

Awards & Exhibitions Continued

Distinguished Architect
Helmut Jahn
City of Milwaukee Art Commission's 1985
Annual Awards
Plaza East Office Center
1985

AIA Chicago Chapter Award
Addition to the Chicago Board of Trade
1984

AISC Award
Addition to the Chicago Board of Trade
1983

AIA Chicago Chapter Award
Area 2 Police Headquarters
1983

Second Annual Award for Distinguished Architecture
Reliance Development Group Inc.
Addition to the Chicago Board of Trade
1982

Arnold W. Brunner Memorial Prize in Architecture
Helmut Jahn
1982

AIA Chicago Chapter Award
Argonne Program Support Facility
1982

ASHRAE Energy Award
De La Garza Career Center
1981

ASHRAE Energy Award
Commonwealth Edison District
Headquarters
1981

ASHRAE Energy Award
State Of Illinois Center
1981

AIA Chicago Chapter Award
De La Garza Career Center
1981

AIA Chicago Chapter Award
Xerox Centre
1980

Young Professional Award
Building Design & Construction Magazine
Rust-Oleum Headquarters
1979

Owens-Corning Fiberglas Energy Conservation Award
Argonne Program Support Facility
1979

AISC Award
Michigan City Library
1979

AISC Award
Rust-Oleum Headquarters
1979

AIA National Honor Award
St Mary's Athletic Facility
1979

AIA Chicago Chapter Award
Rust-Oleum Headquarters
1979

Progressive Architecture Design Citation
Minnesota II
1978

AISC Award
St Mary's Athletic Facility
1978

AIA Chicago Chapter Award
Minnesota II
1978

AIA Chicago Chapter Award
Kansas Convention Center
1978

AIA Chicago Chapter Award
La Lumiere Gymnasium
1978

AIA Chicago Chapter Award
Oak Brook Post Office
1978

AIA Chicago Chapter Award
University of Illinois Agricultural
Engineering Science Building
1978

AIA American Library Association First Honor Award
Michigan City Library
1978

Winner in National Architecture Competition
Minnesota II
1977

Progressive Architecture Design Citation
Xerox Centre
1977

AIA Illinois Council Honor Award
Michigan City Library
1977

AIA Illinois Council Honor Award
St Mary's Athletic Facility
1977

AIA Chicago Chapter Award
Michigan City Library
1977

AIA Chicago Chapter Award
St Mary's Athletic Facility
1977

Progressive Architecture Design Citation
Abu Dhabi Conference City
1976

Prize in International Competition
Abu Dhabi Conference City
1976

AIA Chicago Chapter Award
Auraria Library
1976

Bartelt Award
Kemper Arena
1975

AISC Award
Kemper Arena
1975

AIA National Honor Award
Kemper Arena
1975

AIA Chicago Chapter Award
Kemper Arena
1975

Exhibitions

Building for Air Transportation
Art Institute of Chicago
1995

New Chicago Architecture,
The Chicago Athenaeum
November 1994

Hyatt Amsterdam
ARCAM Galerie, Amsterdam,
The Netherlands
January 1994

New Chicago Architecture Exhibition
Europa-Haus, Fort Canning Tower, Hyatt
Regency Roissy, Messeturm/Messe Halle,
120 North LaSalle, Sony/Berlin
March 1993

Chicago Architecture and Design:
1923–1993
Art Institute of Chicago
May 1993

The Art of Design
Milwaukee, Wisconsin
June 1993

City-Projects
Berlin Pavilion, Berlin, Germany
September 1993

Buenos Aires Biennial of Architecture '93
Recent Work at the Museum of Fine Arts
September 1993

Celebrating 75 Years of Chicago Architecture
The Arts Club of Chicago
January 1992

From Mars to Main Street: America Designs
Washington, DC
November 1992 to December 1993

American Skyscrapers
Helsinki, Finland
March 1993

New Chicago Architecture
The Chicago Athenaeum
January 1991

Helmut Jahn
YKK—Cupples Design Forum, Tokyo, Japan
November 1991

Chicago Architecture
Gulbenkian Foundation
Lisbon, Portugal
1990

The Socially Responsible Environment: US/USSR 1980–1990
Architects Designers Planners for Social Responsibility, USA, and USSR Union of Architects
New York, New York
May 1990

Celebrate Chicago Architecture
Metropolitan Press
Union Station in Washington, DC
June 1990

Terminus to Interchange
The Building Centre Trust, London, England
September 1990

The Art of Design
One Liberty Place, Bank of the Southwest Tower
STA Gallery, Chicago, Illinois
January 1989

Architecture in New York
Columbus Circle, Times Square, Terminalgebäude für AA, North Western JFK
Deutsches Architekturmuseum, Germany
March 1989

Original Unpublished Drawings and Models by Chicago Architectural Club Members
Ruth Volid Gallery, Chicago, Illinois
June 1989

Design USA—A US–USSR Cultural Exchange Exhibition
United States Information Agency, USSR
September 1989

Competitions in Architecture
The Architectural League of New York
New York, New York
September 1989

Tall Buildings
Brisbane, Australia
West Perth, Australia
October 1989

New Chicago Architecture
Metropolitan Press, Chicago, Illinois
November 1989

The Experimental Tradition
The Architectural League, New York, New York
May 1988

New Chicago Skyscrapers
ArchiCenter Gallery, Chicago, Illinois
July 1988

Experimental Skytowers
Rizzoli International Bookstore, Chicago, Illinois
August 1988

The Cities of the World and the Future of the Metropolis
Triennale di Milano, Italy
September 1988

The Postmodern Explained to Children
Bonne Fanten Museum, Maastricht, The Netherlands
November 1988

What Could Have Been: Unbuilt Architecture of the '80s
Dallas Market Center, Dallas, Texas
January 1987

Chicago Architecture Foundation, Chicago, Illinois
December 1987

GA International '87
GA Gallery, Tokyo, Japan
May 1987

Helmut Jahn
Architekturgalerie, Munich, Germany
June 1987

New Chicago Skyscrapers
Merchandise Mart, Chicago, Illinois
July 1987

Helmut Jahn
Paris Art Center, Paris, France
September 1987

Members' Work
The Chicago Architectural Club
Betsy Rosenfield Gallery, Chicago, Illinois
January 1986

Modernism Redux: Critical Alternatives
Grey Art Gallery and Study Center, New York University, New York, New York
February 1986

Vision der Moderne
Deutsches Architekturmuseum, Frankfurt, Germany
June 1986

The National Museum of Modern Art, Tokyo
October 1986

Helmut Jahn
Gallery MA, Tokyo, Japan
October 1986

New Chicago Skyscrapers
Gallery of Design of the Merchandise Mart, Chicago, Illinois
October 1986

Exhibition on Advanced Structures
Syracuse University, Syracuse, New York
January 1985

Vu de l'Interieur ou la Raison de l'Architecture
(Looking from the Inside or the Reason of Architecture)
Paris Biennale, Paris, France
March 1985

150 Years of Chicago Architecture
Museum of Science and Industry, Chicago, Illinois
October 1985

Helmut Jahn
Ballenford Architectural Books and Gallery
Toronto, Ontario, Canada
February 1984

Chicago and New York, More than a Century of Architectural Interaction
The Art Institute of Chicago; The AIA Foundation, The Octagon, Washington, D.C.; Farish Gallery, Rice University, Houston, Texas; The New York Historical Society, New York, New York
March 1984

Opening, Permanent Architectural Collection
Deutsches Architekturmuseum, Frankfurt, Germany
June 1984

Art and... Architecture/Design
Moosart Gallery, Miami, Florida
November 1984

Members' Work
The Chicago Architectural Club
The Art Institute of Chicago, Chicago, Illinois
November 1984

The State of Illinois Center
University of Illinois, Champaign-Urbana, Illinois
December 1984

The Architect's Vision From Sketch to Final Drawing
The Chicago Historical Society, Chicago, Illinois
February 1983

Current Projects
Thomas Beeby, Lawrence Booth, Helmut Jahn, Krueck and Olson, Stanley Tigerman
Young-Hoffman Gallery Chicago, Illinois
February 1983

Awards & Exhibitions Continued

Ornamentalism: The New Decorativeness in Architecture and Design
The Hudson River Museum, New York, New York; Archer M. Huntington Art Gallery, University of Texas, Austin, Texas
March 1983

New Chicago Architecture 1983
The Art Institute of Chicago, Chicago, Illinois
May 1983

Minneapolis Profile 1983
Walker Art Center, Minneapolis, Minnesota
Participant in symposium
May 1983

Tall Buildings
The Southern Chapter, Alberta Association of Architects, Calgary, Alberta, Canada
June 1983

Design USA
Castello Sforzasco in the Sala Viscontea, Milano, Italy
September 1983

Surface and Ornament
Puck Building, New York, New York
October 1983

Contemporary Landscape—from the Horizon of Postmodern Design
The National Museums of Modern Art, Kyoto and Tokyo, Japan
September/December 1985

Competitions Won and Lost
San Francisco AIA Headquarters Gallery, San Francisco, California
October 1983

150 Years of Chicago Architecture
Paris Art Center, Paris, France
October 1983

1992 Chicago World's Fair Design Conference Drawings, New York, Los Angeles, Chicago
The University of Illinois, Chicago Campus, Chicago, Illinois
November 1983

100 Years of Architectural Drawings in Chicago
Illinois Bell Telephone Company, Chicago, Illinois
November 1983

Tops and Members' Work
The Chicago Architectural Club
The Art Institute of Chicago, Chicago, Illinois
November 1983

The Art of Design
University of Milwaukee Fine Arts Galleries, Milwaukee, Wisconsin
October 1983

The Chicago Architectural Club
The Art Institute of Chicago, Chicago, Illinois
August 1982

Chicago Architects Design
The Art Institute of Chicago, Chicago, Illinois
October 1982

Helmet Jahn
School of Architecture, Yale University, New Haven, Connecticut
November 1982

Contemporary Chicago Architecture
Festival of the Arts
Northern Illinois University, DeKalb, Illinois
November 1982

Helmut Jahn
The Fort Worth Art Museum, Fort Worth, Texas
1981

Chicago Architectural Drawing
Frumkin & Struve, Chicago, Illinois
January 1981

The Chicago Architectural Club
Graham Foundation, Chicago, Illinois
March 1981

Chicago International Art Exhibit
Navy Pier, Chicago, Illinois
May 1981

Architecture as Synthesis
Harvard University Graduate School of Design, Cambridge, Massachusetts
December 1981

Arnold W. Brunner Memorial Prize and Exhibit
American Academy and Institute of Arts and Letters, New York, New York
1981/82

City Segments
Walker Art Center, Minneapolis, Minnesota
April 1980

Late Entries to the Chicago Tribune Competition
Museum of Contemporary Art, Chicago, Illinois
May 1980

The Presence of the Past
Biennale, Venice, Italy
June 1980
Paris, France; San Francisco, California
1981–1982

The Architectural Process
Young-Hoffman Gallery, Chicago, Illinois
August 1980

Designing Today for Tomorrow
Architectural League of New York, New York
Participant in symposium
October 1980

25th Annual Progressive Architecture Awards Jury
New York, New York
Participant
1979

Townhouses
Walker Art Center, Minneapolis, Minnesota
Participant in group show
December 1978

State of the Art of Architecture/77
Graham Foundation, Chicago, Illinois
Participant in symposium
October 1977

Chicago 7
Member
1977

Exquisite Corpse
Walter Kelly Gallery, Chicago, Illinois
Participant in group show
December 1977

AIA Chicago Chapter Awards
The Art Institute of Chicago
1974 – 1986

Bibliography

Books

100 Contemporary Architects and their Drawings. Abrams, 1991.

Allen, Gerald & Oliver, Richard. *Architectural Drawing: The Art and the Process*. New York: Whitney Library of Design (imprint of Watson-Guptill Publications) and London: The Architectural Press Ltd, 1981.

American High-Rise Buildings. Tokyo: A + U Publishing Co. Ltd, 1988.

American Skycrapers/Amerikkalaisia Pivenpiirtaejiae. Exhibition catalog. Finland, 1992.

Architecture Chicago Vol. 6: The Divine Detail. Chicago: Chicago Chapter, American Institute of Architects, 1988.

Arnell, Peter & Bickford, Ted (eds). *A Tower for Louisville: The Humana Competition*. New York: Rizzoli International Publications Inc., 1982.

Arnell, Peter & Bickford, Ted (eds). *Southwest Center: The Houston Competition*. New York: Rizzoli International Publications Inc. 1983.

Blaser, Werner. *After Mies*. Von Reinhold Co., 1977.

Blaser, Werner. *Elemental Building Forms*. Germany: Beton-Verlag, 1982.

Blaser, Werner. *Filigree Architecture*. Germany: Wepf & Co., 1980.

Blaser, Werner. *Mies van der Rohe: Continuing the Chicago School of Architecture*. Germany: Birkhauser Verlag, 1981.

Casari, Maurizio & Pavan, Vincenzo (eds). *New Chicago Architecture*. New York: Rizzoli International Publications Inc., 1981.

Chicago and New York: Architectural Interactions. The Art Institute of Chicago, 1984.

Chicago Architects Design: A Century of Architectural Drawings for the Art Institute of Chicago. The Art Institute of Chicago/New York: Rizzoli International Publications Inc., 1982.

Chicago Architecture. Chicago: Chicago Chapter, American Institute of Architects, 1991.

The Chicago Architectural Journal vol. 1. Chicago: The Chicago Architectural Club/ New York: Rizzoli International Publications Inc., 1981.

The Chicago Architectural Journal vol. 2. Chicago: The Chicago Architectural Club/ New York: Rizzoli International Publications Inc., 1982.

The Chicago Architectural Journal vol. 3. Chicago: The Chicago Architectural Club/ New York: Rizzoli International Publications Inc., 1983.

The Chicago Architectural Journal vol. 4. Chicago: The Chicago Architectural Club/ New York: Rizzoli International Publications Inc., 1984.

The Chicago Architectural Journal vol. 5. Chicago: The Chicago Architectural Club/ New York: Rizzoli International Publications Inc., 1985.

The Chicago Architectural Journal vol. 6. Chicago: The Chicago Architectural Club/ New York: Rizzoli International Publications Inc., 1987.

City-Projekte. Berlin, 1993.

Competitions vol. 1. Louisville, Kentucky: 1991.

Contemporary American Architects. Germany: Benedikt Taschen GmbH, 1993.

Contemporary Masterworks. St James Press, 1992.

De Vito, Alfredo. *Innovative Management Techniques for Architectural Design and Construction*. New York: Whitney Library of Design/Watson-Guptill Publications, 1984.

Diamonstein, Barbara Lee (ed.). *American Architecture Now II*. Forward by Paul Goldberger. New York: Rizzoli International Publications Inc., 1985.

DLW Nachrichten 65/1985. Germany: DLW Architektenforum, 1985.

Emanuel, Muriel (ed.). *Contemporary Architects*. St Martin's Press, 1980.

Fraser, Iain & Henmi, Rod. *Envisioning Architecture—An Analysis of Drawing*. 1994.

From Mars to Main Street: America Designs. Exhibition catalog. Washington, DC: 1993.

Für Sport und Mode: Munich Order Center. Germany: Institut fur Internationale Architektur-Dokumentation, 1993.

Glibota, Ante (ed.). *10 Years of Chicago Architecture*. Paris: Paris Art Center, 1985.

Glibota, Ante (ed.). *Helmut Jahn Modern Romantic*. Paris: Paris Art Center, 1987.

Goldberger, Paul. *The Skyscraper*. New York: Alfred A. Knopf, 1981.

Grube, Pran & Schultze. *100 Years of Architecture in Chicago*. Follet Co., 1976.

Helmut Jahn 1982–1992. Tokyo: A + U Publishing Co., 1992.

Helmut Jahn Airports. Basel: Birkhäuser Verlag, 1991.

Helmut Jahn—Extra Edition. Tokyo: A + U Publishing Co. Ltd, 1986.

Herbert, Daniel M. *Architectural Study Drawings*. 1993.

Hotel Kempinski—Extra Edition. Tokyo: A + U Publishing Co. Ltd, 1995.

Huxtable, Ada Louise. *The Tall Building Artistically Reconsidered: The Search for a Skyscraper Style*. New York: Pantheon Books, 1984.

Ideas and Ideologies in the Late Twentieth Century. American Architecture, Paul Heyer, 1993.

International Architecture Yearbook. Melbourne, Australia: The Images Publishing Group, 1995.

Jahn, Helmut, Kraus, Patrick & Jeschenko, Rudolf. *Helmut Jahn, Building Identity*. Düsseldorf, Germany: ECON, Executive Verlags GmbH, 1992.

Jencks, Carl. *Late Modern Architecture*. New York: Rizzoli International Publications Inc., 1980.

Bibliography Continued

Joedicke, Joachim Andreas (ed.). *Helmut Jahn—Design of a New Architecture*. Stuttgart, Zurich: Karl Kramer Verlag, 1986.

Klotz, Heinrich (ed.). *Die Revision der Moderne: Postmoderne Architektur 1960–1980*. Germany: Prestel, 1984.

Klotz, Heinrich (ed.). *Vision der Moderne—Das Prinzip Konstruktion*. Frankfurt: Deutsches Architekturmuseum/Prestel-Verlag, 1986.

Klotz, Heinrich. *Jahrbuch Fur Architektur 1981/82*. Germany: Deutsches Architektur Museum/Friedr. Viewg. & Sohn, 1981.

Klotz, Heinrich. *Jahrbuch Fur Architektur 1983*. Germany: Deutsches Architektur Museum/Friedr. Viewg. & Sohn, 1983.

Klotz, Heinrich. *Moderne und Postmoderne*. Germany: Friedr. Viewg. & Sohn, 1984.

Krantz, Les (ed.). *American Architects*. New York, 1989.

Laine, Christian K. (ed.). *The Chicago Architectural Annual 1985*. Chicago: Metropolitan Press Publications, 1985.

Lampugnani, Vittorio Magnago. *Architecture in Our Century in Drawings: Utopia and Reality*. Germany: Verlag Gerd Hatje, 1982.

Lauber, M. (ed.). "Beyond the Modern Movement." *Harvard Review*, vol. 1. MIT Press, 1980.

Mardaga, Pierre (ed.). *Biennale de Paris Architecture 1985*. Paris, France.

Miller, Nory. *Helmut Jahn*. New York: Rizzoli International Publications Inc., 1986.

Münchener Order Center MOC: Architekten Murphy/Jahn. Munich: Stahl Informations Zentrum, 1993.

Nelson, Susan R. (ed.). *Groundworks: North American Underground Projects 1980 to 1989*. Washington, DC: 1989.

New York Architektur. Munich: Prestel Verlag, 1989.

Portoghesi, Paolo. *Postmodern: The Architecture of the Postindustrial Society*. New York: Rizzoli International Publications Inc., 1984.

Quaternario 90. Milan, Italy: Electa, 1990.

The Sky's The Limit. Chicago: Art Institute of Chicago, 1991.

A Style for the Year 2001. Tokyo: Shinkenchiku Co. Ltd, 1985.

Sourcebook of Contemporary North American Architecture. New York: Van Nostrand Reinhold, 1989.

Thorndike, Joseph J. Jr (ed.). *Three Centuries of Notable American Architects*. New York: American Heritage Publishing Co. Inc., 1981.

Vision of the Modern. London: UIA Journal of Architectural Theory and Criticism, 1988.

Wirth, Harry J. *The Art of Design 2*. Milwaukee, Wisconsin: 1993.

Periodicals

"1990 AISC Architectural Awards of Excellence." *Modern Steel Construction* (November/December 1990). (United Airlines, One Liberty Place)

"2000 and Beyond." *Progressive Architecture* (December 1985). (State of Illinois Center)

"27th Annual PA Awards." *Progressive Architecture* (January 1980).

"750 Lexington Avenue at 59th Street." *Real Estate Forum* (New York, December 1986).

"88 Field Street." *Architect & Builder* (Johannesburg, July 1986). (362 West Street)

"A Pioneer of Chicago's West Loop." *Building Design and Construction* (September 1988). (Northwestern Atrium Center)

"A Skyscraper on the Corner." *l'Arca* (June 1993). (Fountain Square West)

"A Tale of Four New Towers and What They Tell of Trends." *Architecture* (May 1988). (One Liberty Place)

"A Tall Order—The 31-Story Oakbrook Terrace Tower." *DuPage Profile* (January 21/22, 1987). (Oakbrook Terrace Tower)

"A Third Philadelphia Plan—A Critical View." *Architecture* (October 1988). (Liberty Place)

"Abu Dhabi Conference City." *Progressive Architecture* (January 1977).

"Abu Dhabi/UAE." *Domus* (Milan, June 1979).

"Aerger mit der Presse." *Newmag* (Germany, February 1992).

"Amerika im Streiflicht." *Schweizer Ingenieur und Architekt* (Switzerland, no. 1/2, January 11, 1990). (United Airlines Terminal)

"Analysis of Planned and Completed Projects by C.F. Murphy Associates." *Bauen + Wohnen* (Zurich, September 1974).

"And Now the Tallest of the Tall." *Time* (December 2, 1985). (Television City)

"Arch Angles." *Architecture Journal* (vol. 183, no. 8, February 1986). (Galveston Arches)

"Architects for the 1990's." *Fortune* (June 22, 1987). (North Western Terminal, Park Avenue Tower)

"Architecture as a Corporate Asset." *Business Week* (October 4, 1982). (Addition to the Chicago Board of Trade)

"Architecture Peak Performance." *Chicago Tribune* (October 20, 1991).

"Architecture: Chicago's Skyscraping Romantic—Helmut Jahn." *Interview* (September 1983). (North Western Terminal, Bank of the Southwest Tower)

"Architecture: Helmut Jahn." *Architectural Digest* (March 1984). (Eagle River Wisconsin House)

"Architecture—The Temple of Marketing." *The New Republic* (October 26, 1987). (United Airlines Terminal)

"Architektur: Die grossen Wurfe von morgen" *Stern* (Germany, November 1989).

"Argonne Program Support Facility." *Progressive Architecture* (April 1979).

"Auraria Learning Center." *AIA Journal* (September 1979).

"Auraria Library." *A + U* (Tokyo, October 1978).

"Auraria Library." *Architectural Record* (November 1977).

"Auraria Library." *Domus* (Milan, July 1977).

"Auraria Library." *Inland Architect* (August 1976, November 1976).

"A Babel of New Towers." *Chicago* magazine (April 1984).

"Barone von High Tech." *Epoca* (November 1987). (United Airlines Terminal, State of Illinois Center, O'Hare Rapid Transit Station)

"The Battle of Starship Chicago." *Time* (Design section, February 4, 1985). (State of Illinois Center)

"A Berlin Story." *Interiors* (May 1993).

"The Best Building in Town?" *San Diego* magazine (October 1989). (Great American Plaza)

"The Best of '87—Architecture." *Business Week* (January 11, 1988). (One Liberty Place, United Airlines Terminal)

"Best of Chicago—Best New Skyscraper." *Chicago* magazine (January 1983). (One South Wacker)

"Big Jahn, Offices, Chicago." *Architectural Review* (London, April 1981). (One South Wacker, Xerox Centre)

"Board of Trade Addition: A New Synthesis." *Inland Architect* (September 1980).

"A Bold New Breed of Buidings is Reaching Towards the Skies." *Smithsonian* (October 1983). (One South Wacker, Xerox Centre, Bank of the Southwest Tower)

"The Building of the Year 2000." *Inland Architect* (May 1980).

"Building on a Tradition of Excellence." *Advertising Age* (March 1983).

"Building the New Germany." *Blueprint* (April 1993).

"C.F. Murphy Associates Five Projects." *GA Document 1* (Tokyo, Spring 1980).

"Can Chicago Architecture Live Up to Its Past?." *The New Art Examiner* (January 1984). (One South Wacker, State of Illinois Center, Addition to the Chicago Board of Trade, Xerox Centre, North Western Terminal)

"CFMA Office Building." *A + U* (Tokyo, April 1980).

"CFMA Portfolio." *Domus* (Milan, April 1978).

"CFMA Portfolio." *L'Architectura* (Milan, December 1977).

"CFMA Portfolio." *Progressive Architecture* (July 1978).

"CFMA Portfolio." *The Architectural Review* (London, October 1977).

"The Changing Skins of Helmut Jahn." *AIA Journal* (October 1981).

"Chicago Architecture After Mies." *Critical Inquiry* (University of Chicago, Winter 1979).

"The Chicago Chapter/AIA 1980 Distinguished Building Awards." *Inland Architect* (December 1980).

"Chicago Design: In Search of a New Order." *Interiors* (May 1983). (Murphy/Jahn)

"Chicago Library Entries Unveiled." *Progressive Architecture* (July 1988). (Chicago Public Library Competition)

"Chicago Skyscrapers: Romanticism and Reintegration." *Domus* (September 1984). (Addition to the Chicago Board of Trade)

"Chicago Story..." (Tribune Competition) *Horizon* (July 1980).

"Chicago Team Wins Minnesota Competition" *Progressive Architecture* (April 1977).

"Chicago". *Merian* (Germany, August 1990).

"Chicago-Design." *Town & Country* (September 1990).

"Chicago." *Departures* (October/November 1991).

"Chicago." *Holland Herald* (The Netherlands, vol. 17, no. 12, 1982). (Xerox Centre, State of Illinois Center, North Western Terminal)

"Chicago." *Progressive Architecture* (June 1980).

"Chicago: Architecture City." *Habitat Ufficio* (Milan, April/May 1993). (Murphy/Jahn, Munich Airport Center)

"Chicago: La Griglia L'Infinito." *Domus* (March 1982). (Addition to the Chicago Board of Trade)

"Chicago—Home of Many Greats." *CCAIA Focus* (October 1991).

"City Segments/Exhibition." *Inland Architect* (June 1980).

"Color and Geometry in Wisconsin Woods." *Architecture* (May 1984).

"Competitors Helmut Jalm." *Competitions* (vol. 4, Spring 1994).

"The Constructional Ideas of Helmut Jahn: Paris Art Center Exhibit." *Inland Architect* (January/February 1988).

"Crosby Kemper Arena." *AIA Journal* (April 1976).

"Crossroads Berlin." *The Architectural Review* (January 1993).

Bibliography Continued

"De architectuur van het succes." *Archis* (Amsterdam, May 1986). (State of Illinois Center, Addition to the Chicago Board, One South Wacker, Park Avenue Tower, Humana Competition)

"A Decade for Architecture." *Dialogue* (March 1992).

"Deja Vu: Helmut Jahn in Cincinnati." *Inland Architect* (September/October 1990).

"Der Grosse Hochmut—Helmut Jahn" *Bunte Heft 1* (Germany, December 29, 1988).

"Der Messeturm in Frankfurt." *DBZ* (Germany, January 1992).

"Der Messeturm." *Pflasterstrand* (Germany, September 1990).

"Der Schnellste Colt Imganzen Westen: Jahn-Bau State of Illinois Center in Chicago." *Der Spiegel* (Germany, no. 24, June 10, 1985). (State of Illinois Center)

"Der Turm zeugt vom asthetischen Willen der Stadt." *Galleria* (February 1989). (Messe Frankfurt)

"Der Wolkenkratzer." *German Esquire* (July 1988). (Messe Frankfurt, State of Illinois Center, Xerox Centre, O'Hare Rapid Transit Station, One South Wacker)

"Design Direction: Looking for What is Missing." *AIA Journal* (May 1978).

"Design/Projects Feature: To Be Continued." *Progressive Architecture* (March 1990). (750 Lexington, Park Avenue Tower, One Liberty Place, Messeturm/Messehalle, 120 N. LaSalle, Ku-Damm 70, North Loop, Raffles Place and Collier Quay, 1111 Brickell, Victoria City, Munich Airport Center, JFK Terminal/American Airlines)

"Designs for Living." *Newsweek* (November 1978).

"Design—The Best of 1988: United Airlines Terminal O'Hare International Airport, Helmut Jahn Architect." *Esquire* (December 1988).

"Die Grossen Fun." *Scala* (Italy, September/October 1992).

"Don't talk build." *Living* (February 1993). (Sony Center Berlin)

"Donald Trump's Lofty Ambition." *Newsweek* (December 2, 1985). (Television City)

"Due progetti di Murphy/Jahn." *l'Arca* (January 1993). (Yokohama Waterfront PJ, Tokyu-Shibuya Tower)

"Eauen Sie mir ein Buerohaus in dem Menschen gern arbeiten!" *P.M.* magazine (Germany, January 19, 1990). (State of Illinois Center)

"Echos of the Past Visions for the Present—Best of '87." *Time* (January 4, 1988). (United Airlines Terminal)

"The Economics of Image Building." *Building Design and Construction* (March 1989). (Liberty Place, Oak Brook Terrace Tower)

"Ein Amerikaner am Rhein: Mannheimer Versicherungsbau von Helmut Jahn." *STEINtime* (Germany, September 1992).

"Ein Mann Baut Bunt." ("A Man Builds Bountifully.") *Stern* magazine (Germany, no. 40, September 26, 1985). (Southwest Center, State of Illinois Center, One South Wacker, Shand Morahan Plaza, O'Hare Rapid Transit Station, Oakbrook Post Office, Penn Yards)

"Eingangsbau und Messehalle 1 in Frankfurt/Main" *Glasforum* (Germany, December 1989).

"El encanto de la imitacion." *Arquitectura Viva* (Buenos Aires, March 1994). (Liberty Place)

"Emerging Skyline." *Domus* (Milan, February 1986). (Television City, South Ferry Plaza)

"European Forecast." *Architecture* (September 1990).

"The Excitement Is Building." *Express* (June 1981).

"Facts About: The Terminal for Tomorrow." *Vis a Vis* (August 1987). (United Airlines Terminal)

"Flughafen O'Hare in Chicago —Terminal 1." *Architektur* (Germany, July 1991).

"The Flash Gordon of American Architecture." *Architecture Bulletin* (June 1983).

"Form Follows Fantasy" *Time* (Design section, February 17, 1986).

"Fourth District Courts Building/John Marshall Courts Building." *A + U* (September 1979).

"Frankfurt Campanile." *Architectural Record* (February 1993).

"Frankfurt's Messeturm." *l'Arca* (September 1990).

"Genesis of a Tower: Helmut Jahn Drawings." *AIA Technology* (Fall 1983). (Bank of the Southwest Tower)

"Giganten Desunendlichen." *Ambiente* (Germany, January 1992).

"Glass Highlights Design of Bank/Hotel Complex." *Building Design and Construction* (March 1983). (First Source Center)

"The Glittering City of Helmut Jahn." *Chicago* magazine (February 1986).

"Going for the Glitz." *House and Garden* (March 1988). (United Airlines Terminal, One Liberty Place)

"A Grand Gateway." *Progressive Architecture* (November 1987). (United Airlines Terminal)

"H. Roe Bartle Exhibition Hall." *Detail* (Germany, July/August 1980).

"Half Time—Cerebrating 75 Years of Chicago Architecture." Exhibition catalog. Arts Club of Chicago (January 1992).

"Hauptsache Kultur-Berlin: Verkauf Der Hauptstadt." *Forbes* (April 1992).

"Helmut Jahn (Murphy/Jahn)." *A + U* (Tokyo, November 1983). (Addition to the Chicago Board of Trade, One South Wacker, State of Illinois Center, 701 Avenue South, 362 West Street, Bank of the Southwest Tower, 11 Diagonal Street, MGIC Plaza East, John Deere Harvester Works Office, Shand Morahan Office Building, Greyhound Terminal, Chicago-O'Hare International Airport Development Program, North Western Terminal, Wilshire/Midvale)

"Helmut Jahn El Liberty Place de Filadelfia." *Diseno y Decoracion en la Argentina.* (June 1993).

"Helmut Jahn Four Towers 1978–82." *Architectural Review* (no. 7/8, London, 1983). (Addition to the Chicago Board of Trade, One South Wacker, Humana, Bank of the Southwest Tower)

"Helmut Jahn in Mannheim." *Office Design* (April 1993).

"Helmut Jahn Krafzt Wolken." *Frankfurter Allgemeine* magazine (Germany, December 12, 1986). (Messe Frankfurt, State of Illinois Center, One South Wacker, Shand Morahan Plaza, 70 Lexington, O'Hare Rapid Transit Station)

"Helmut Jahn mit Wolken-Kratzen zum Erflog." *Das Beste aus Reader's Digest* (December 12, 1986). (Messe Frankfurt)

"Helmut Jahn on Architecture as Synthesis." *Harvard Graduate School of Design News* (Winter 1982).

"Helmut Jahn Puts the State Under Glass." *Chicago* magazine (July 1980).

"Helmut Jahn Romances New York A Tough Town." *Crain's Chicago Business* (August 1, 1988). (City Spire, 750 Lexington, 425 Lexington, Park Avenue Tower, 300 E. 82nd St)

"Helmut Jahn State of Illinois Center in Chicago." *Architektur* (Germany, October 1991).

"Helmut Jahn Topples the Box." *Architect & Builder* (Johannesburg, June 1982). (Addition to the Chicago Board of Trade, North Western Terminal, No. 11 Diagonal Street, St Mary's Athletic Facility, Kemper Arena, Xerox Centre, State of Illinois Center)

"Helmut Jahn's Latest Glass-Clad Building in Chicago." *Architect & Builder* (Johannesburg, November 1984). (One South Wacker)

"Helmut Jahn's Tall Buildings." *Art* (October 1990).

"Helmut Jahn, C.F. Murphy Associates." *GA Document 1* (April 1987). (State of Illinois Center, Xerox Centre, Chicago Board of Trade Addition, One South Wacker, North Western Terminal)

"Helmut Jahn." *Bauwelt* (Germany, May 1992).

"Helmut Jahn." *GA Document GA International '89* (1989). (Messeturm)

"Helmut Jahn." *Gentlemen's Quarterly* (September 1983). (One South Wacker, North Western Terminal)

"Helmut Jahn." *Mensch & Buro* (Germany, March 1990).

"Helmut Jahn: Building for the Future." *The Rotarian* (November 1992).

"Helmut Jahn: The Building of a Legend." *New Art Examiner* (November 1987).

"Helmut Jahn—A La Conquete D'Un Monde Nouveau." *Connaissance des Arts* (Paris, December 1987). (North Western Terminal, United Airlines Terminal, Messe Frankfurt)

"Helmut Jahn—Messeturm." *Bunte* (Germany, March 1994).

"High Flight—United Gambles and Wins at O'Hare." *Inland Architect* (September/October 1988). (United Airlines Terminal)

"High Rise Projects." *Bauen + Wohnen* (June 1981). (Xerox Centre, De La Garza Career Center, Chicago Board of Trade Addition, One South Wacker, North Western Terminal, State of Illinois Center)

"High-Rise Hard Sell." *New York* magazine (March 11, 1985). (425 Lexington, Park Avenue Tower)

"High-Tech Expansion: Chicago-O'Hare International Airport Development Program." *Architectural Record* (May 1985).

"High-Tech: Britain v. America." *The Architectural Review* (August 1983). (Argonne Program Support Facility, First Source Center)

"The Hitachi Tower and Caltex House." *l'Arca* (March 1994).

"Hochhaus Messe Frankfurt." Bibliographisches Institut & F.A. Brockhaus AG Band 10, 1989.

"Hochhauser fur Frankfurt." *Baumeister* (January 1987). (Messe Frankfurt)

"Hot Frankfurters" *Commerce in Germany* (Germany, no. 6, September 1989). (Messe Frankfurt)

"Hotel Hyatt Regency Roissy." *Techniques & Architecture* (Special edition, 1993).

"How Helmut Jahn is Changing the Face of Chicago." *Crain's Chicago Business* (November 9, 1981).

"I want to be in America." *German Vogue* (Germany, April 1992).

"Illinois Center." *Architectural Review* (December 1980).

"Im Bauch der Riesen." *Architektur Innenarchitektur Technischer Ausbau* (Germany, October 1989).

"Inside Helmut Jahn's State of Illinois Triumph—A Search for Excellence." *Interiors* (Cover story, May 1985). (State of Illinois Center, CTA Station—O'Hare, United Airlines Terminal, Murphy/Jahn Cupola, Plaza East Office Center, 425 Lexington, City Center, Park Avenue Tower)

"Inside the Livable City." *Inland Architect* January/February 1989). (Addition to the Chicago Board of Trade, State of Illinois Center)

"An Island Outside the Paris Gates" *l'Arca* (July/August 1991). (Hyatt Regency Roissy, Ku-Damm 70)

Bibliography Continued

"It's What's Outside That Counts" *Inland Architect* July/August 1991). (Wilshire/Westwood)

"Jahn Building Identities." *High Touch* (no. 2, 1990). (State of Illinois Center)

"Jahn in the Loop." *On the Boards Architecture* (February 1990). (550 Madison, Savings of America Tower, Wells & Lake Office Tower, North Loop Block 37, Project J)

"Jahn's Bold Designs Taking Root in West Suburban Soil." *Crain's Chicago Business* (March 24, 1986). (MetroWest, Oakbrook Terrace Tower)

"Jahn's Chicago 1: Board of Trade", "Jahn's Chicago 2: One South Wacker." The Sixth Annual Review of New American Architecture. *AIA Journal* (May 1983).

"Jahn's Designs Shatter the Box." *Engineering News Record* (October 8, 1981).

"Jeu d'Enveloppes, Un Rond dans L'eau." *Techniques & Architecture* (Paris, September 1984). (First Source Center, Argonne Program Support Facilities)

"Kansas City Convention Center." *Domus* (Milan, February 1979).

"Kemper Arena." *Architectural Record* (March 1976).

"Kemper Arena." *Detail* (Germany, May/June 1979).

"Kemper Arena." *Domus* (Milan, July 1976).

"Kemper Arena." *Inland Architect* (June 1976).

"Kemper Arena/H. Roe Bartle." *AIA Journal* (March 1979).

"Kempinski Hotel." *l'Arca* (January 1995).

"Ku Damm 70 Berlin" *Progressive Architecture* (April 1989).

"Ku Damm 70, Ku Damm 119, Victoria Berlin and Sony Center Berlin." *Nikkei Architecture* (Tokyo, December 20, 1993).

"La Lumiere Gymnasium." *Domus* (January 1980).

"La Torre Della Fiera Di Francoforte" *Abitare* (Milan, no. 274, May 1989). (Messe Frankfurt)

"Late Entries." *Progressive Architecture* (June 1980).

"Late Postmodern—The End of Style." *Art in America* (June 1987).

"Latest Murphy/Jahn." *World Architecture* (London, March 1994).

"Look What Landed in the Loop." *Architecture* (November 1985). (State of Illinois Center)

"Made by Helmut Jahn." *Architektur Innenarchitektur Technischer Ausbau* (Germany, December 1992).

"Man of Dreams." *BMW magazine* (Germany, January 1993).

"The Master Builder." *GQ* (Cover story, May 1985). (State of Illinois Center, Xerox Centre, One South Wacker)

"Messehalle 1 Frankfurt/Main" *Dokumentation Detail* (Germany, August/September 1989).

"Messeturm and Messe Halle." *Nikkei Architecture* (Tokyo, October 1991).

"The Messe Tower/Messe Halle in Frankfurt." *l'Industria Delle Costruzioni* (March 1994).

"Messeturm Frankfurt." *Ambiente* (Germany, October 1992).

"Messeturm." *Architektur Innenarchitektur Technischer Ausbau* (Germany, cover story, April 1989).

"Metaalnijverheid met architect Helmut Jahn in Rotterdam." *UGM* (May 1991).

"Michigan City Library." *Building Design and Construction* (December 1977).

"Michigan City Library; St Mary's Athletic Facility." *GA Document* (Special Issue 1979–1980).

"Minnesota II." *Architecture Minnesota* (January/February 1978).

"Minnesota II." *Engineering News Record* (March 1977).

"Minnesota II." *Progressive Architecture* (January 1979).

"MOC—Munchner—Order Center." *DBZ* (Germany, February 1994).

"Monroe Centre." *Inland Architect* (October 1977).

"Monroe Centre." *Progressive Architecture* (January 1978).

"Movement and Color as Themes." *Architecture* (May 1987). (O'Hare Rapid Transit Station)

"Munich Order Center and Mannheimer Lebensversicherung." *Aprire* (no. 2, 1993).

"Munich Order Center." *l'Arca* (February 1994).

"Murphy y Jahn en la feria." *Arquitectura Viva* (Buenos Aires, no. 8, October 1989). (Messeturm)

"Murphy/Jahn Profile." *Inland Architect* (May/June 1992).

"Murphy/Jahn." *A + U* (Tokyo, February 1983). (First Source Center, Argonne National Laboratories Chicago Branch/Department of Energy, Area 2 Police Center, United States Post Office)

"Murphy/Jahn." *A + U* (Tokyo, January 1986). (State of Illinois Center, 10 Columbus Circle)

"Murphy/Jahn." *World Construction and Engineering* (vol. 2, no. 10, Tokyo, June 1983). (Bank of the Southwest Tower, Addition to the Chicago Board of Trade)

"Murphy/Jahn." *World Construction and Engineering* (vol. 2, no. 12, Tokyo, August 1983). (11 Diagonal St, One South Wacker)

"Murphy/Jahn: State of Illinois Center." *A + U* (January 1984).

"Murphy/Jahn—Recent works and Projects." *GA Document 7* (September 1983). (State of Illinois Center, Oak Brook Post Office, First Source Center, Argonne Program Support Facility, Addition to the Chicago Board of Trade, One South Wacker, Bank of the Southwest Tower, 11 Diagonal Street, 701 Fourth Avenue South, Greyhound Terminal, 362 West Street, Americana Plaza, Shand Morahan Plaza, Wilshire/Midvale, North Loop Block F)

"New Chicago Architecture." *Inland Architect* (May/June 1983). (Bank of the Southwest Tower)

"New Chicago Projects" *Metropolitan Review* (September/October 1989). (North Loop Block 37, Lake and Wells Office Tower, Wells and Lake Office Tower)

"New Departures." *Designers' Journal* (vol. 42, November 1988). (United Airlines Terminal)

"New Designs and Directions at C.F. Murphy Associates." *Architectural Record* (July 1979).

"A New Era Dawns for First Source." *Corporate Design* (November/December 1982). (First Source Center)

"New Wall System Weds Diverse Materials." *Building Design and Construction* (March 1986). (Shand Morahan Plaza)

"A New Trump Card." *Inland Architect* (January 2, 1986). (Television City)

"North Loop Block 37" *Inland Architect* (September/October 1989).

"North Loop Block 37." *l'Arca* (May 1991).

"North Western Center." *Arquitectura* (Buenos Aires, February 1993).

"North Western Terminal." *Bunte* (Germany, no. 6, March 2, 1983).

"Nur Mut zum Streit schafft die ganz grosse Architektur." *Inpulse* (Germany, March 1992).

"The O'Hare Station—Last Link to the Loop." *Inland Architect* (July/August 1985).

"O'Hare United Terminal" *Bauwelt* (Germany, no. 12, March 24, 1989).

"Oben Hui Unten Pfui." *Bauwelt* (Germany, July 1993).

"On Visability Travel and Transformation The Questions of Northwestern Atrium." *Inland Architect* (May/June 1988).

"One Liberty Place, Two Liberty Place, City Spire, Messe Tower." *Real Estate Forum* (May 1988).

"One South Wacker." *Inland Architect* (September 1980).

"Opinion." *Inland Architect* (November 1974).

"Orizzontale/Verticale." *l'Arca* (September 1991). (1111 Brickel Avenue, Project J, Stuttgart Berliner Platz)

"Pa Vilhao de Exposicoes em Munique." *Arquitectura Urbanisma* (Buenos Aires, October/November 1993). (Munich Order Center)

"Pahlavi National Library." *Domus* (Milan, August 1978).

"Prima Donnas on the Landscape—Paul Goldberger on the Indulgence of Postmodernism." *The New Art Examiner* (February 1989). (One Liberty Place)

"Private Residence Eagle River Wisconsin." *GA Houses 17* (January 1985).

"Profile: Chicago Seven, The Exquisite Corpse." *A + U* (Tokyo, July 1978). (Helmut Jahn, C.F. Murphy Associates)

"Prominent Persons in High Tech Architecture—Helmut Jahn." *SD*—*Space Design* (January 1985). (Parktown, Chicago O'Hare International Airport Development Program, 362 West Street)

"Recent Works of Chicago 7." *Architectural Review* (June 1980).

"Reordering the Suburbs." *Progressive Architecture* (May 1989). (Oak Brook Terrace Tower)

"Residence in Eagle River." *A + U* (Tokyo, July 1985).

"Residence—Eagle River Wisconsin U.S.A. Murphy/Jahn." *L'Architecture D'Aujourd'hui* (April 1984).

"Rise to the Top—The Success of Chicago Architect Helmut Jahn." *Metropolis New York* (March 1986).

"Rust-Oleum Corporate Headquarters." *Baumeister* (Germany, September 1980).

"The Savings of America Tower." *l'Arca* (May 1994).

"Screenwall." *Deutsche Bauzeitung* (Germany, July 1991). (Kempinski Hotel)

"Shall We Dance—The Suburban Context of Oakbrook Terrace Tower." *Inland Architect* (November/December 1988).

"The Sky's the Limit." *Newsweek* (November 8, 1982). (Bank of the Southwest Tower, Xerox Centre, Bank of the Southwest Tower, Xerox Centre, State of Illinois Center, North Western Terminal)

"Skyscraper View." *Design Quarterly* (no. 140, Summer 1988). (One Liberty Place)

"Skyscrapers and the City." *Chicago History* Winter 1983/84. (State of Illinois Center, Bank of the Southwest Tower)

"Skyscrapers: Above the Crowd." *National Geographic* (February 1989). (One Liberty Place, Helmut Jahn)

"Snake Skin Skyscrapers." *Domus* (Milan, April 1981). (Xerox Centre, Addition to the Chicago Board of Trade, North Western Terminal)

"Soaring Spaces that Celebrate Travel." *Architecture* (May 1988). (United Airlines Terminal 1)

"Sony-Wettbewerb." *Bauwelt* (Germany, October 1992).

Space Design (February 1983). (State of Illinois Center, Argonne Program Support Facility)

"Special Export, World Comes to Chicago to Draft a Tall One." *Commercial Real Estate Magazine Sun Times* (Spring 1994).

Bibliography Continued

"St Mary's Athletic Facility." *Architectural Record* (April 1979).

"Star on Skyline." *San Diego County Los Angeles Times* (October 1991).

"Starchitects." *Chicago Tribune* magazine (January 18, 1987). (State of Illinois Center, Xerox Centre, One South Wacker, Two Energy Center, One Liberty Place, Messe Frankfurt, New York projects)

"State of Illinois Center." *GA Document 13* (Tokyo, November 1985).

"State of Illinois Center." *Progressive Architecture* (February 1981).

"The State of Space." *Inland Architect* (March/April 1987). (State of Illinois Center, 701 Fourth Avenue South)

"Strutture Metropolitane." *l'Arca* (July/August 1992). (United Airlines Terminal, JFK Terminal)

"Tall Tower for Texas." *Time* (Design section, November 8, 1982). (Bank of the Southwest Tower, Addition to the Chicago Board of Trade, Xerox Centre)

Techniques & Architecture (September 8, 1981). (State of Illinois Center, Xerox Centre, One South Wacker, Chicago Board of Trade, North Western Terminal)

"Television City a New York" *l'Arca* (March 1987).

"Television City." *Architect & Builder* (Johannesburg, May 1986).

"Terminal of the Future." *ID* (January/February 1988). (United Airlines Terminal)

"Teutonisches Wunderkind." *Der Spiegel* (Germany, no. 27, July 5, 1982).

"Three Designs by Murphy/Jahn." *Architectural Record* (December 1981). (North Western Terminal Project, Railway Exchange Building Renovation, O'Hare Rapid Transit Station)

"Three New Designs by C.F. Murphy Associates." *Architectural Record* (August 1980).

"Times Square Project New York, New York, USA Design." *GA Document* (Spring 1987).

"Today's Towers: Reaching for New Heights." *American Arts* (May 1983). (Bank of the Southwest Tower, Humana Corporation Competition)

"Tokyo Teleport Town." *l'Arca* (December 1991).

"Toward Romantic Hi Tech." *Architectural Record* (January 1983). (Area 2 Police Headquarters, Argonne Program Support Facility, First Source Center)

"The Tribune Competition 1922/1980." *Inland Architect* (May 1980).

"Turm-Vater Jahn." *Manager Privat* (Hamburg, May 1986). (Television City)

"U-Bahn Station 'O'Hare' in Chicago Il. USA." *Architektur + Wettbewerbe* (Germany, no. 134, June 1988). (O'Hare Rapid Transit)

"U.S. Architectural Firms Scale New Heights in Pursuit of Project Spawned by Asia's Boom." *The Asian Wall Street Journal Weekly* (March 1994).

"United Airlines Terminal: Best of Category." *ID* (Annual Design Review, July/August 1988).

"United Airlines." *The Canadian Architect* (Canada, June/July 1991).

"United Airlines—O'Hare Framed for Tomorrow." *Modern Steel Construction* (no. 5, September/October 1987). (United Airlines Terminal)

"United's Crystal Palace." *Air & Space Smithsonian* (October/November 1988). (United Airlines Terminal)

"Unschuld verloren." *Der Spiegel* (Germany, no. 14, March 31, 1986). (Messe Frankfurt)

"Urbanes Drama." *Der Spiegel* (Germany, August 1992).

"The Uses of Glass." *Progressive Architecture* (March 1989). (United Airlines Terminal O'Hare International Airport)

"Vision in Glass." *Eckelt* (Germany, December 1993).

"Vom MUC zum MOC." *Bauwelt* (Germany, July 1993).

"What's Next?." *AIA Journal* (May 1980).

"Why Europe's New Skyline is Looking So American." *Business Week* (August 15, 1988). (Messe Frankfurt)

"Wie man mit Beton den Himmel erobert: Der Frankfurter Messeturm." *Frankfurter Allgemeine* magazine (Germany, no. 16, vol April 20, 1990, Heft 529).

"Working Abroad." *Architecture* (September 1993).

"Works of Murphy/Jahn." *A + U* (Tokyo, October 1985). (11 Diagonal Street, 701 Fourth Avenue South, Plaza East, College of Du Page, Shand Morahan Office Headquarters, O'Hare Rapid Transit, University of Illinois Agricultural/Engineering Science Building)

"Xerox Centre." *AIA Journal* (May 1981).

"Xerox Centre." *GA Document 3* (April 1981).

"Xerox Centre." *Progressive Architecture* (December 1980).

Acknowledgments

The work in this book was made **possible** through the efforts of the **Senior Personnel: Sam Scaccia, Philip Castillo, Brian O'Connor, Rainer Schildknecht, Martin F. Wolf, Gordon Beckman, Steven S. Cook, John S Durbrow, Susan Froelich, Scott Pratt, Keith H. Palmer, Dieter Zabel, Edward P. Wilkas, Mark Joshua Frisch, Sanford E. Gorshow, Stephen Kern, Steven M. Nilles, Thomas M. Chambers, Stephen Cavanaugh and Gregg Leoscher; Consulting Architects: Charles Bostick, Fritz Ludwig, Lothar Pascher, Raimond Schöck and Former Senior Personnel: Daniel Dolan, James Goettsch, Robert Goldberg, James M. Stevenson and Dennis Recek.**

Through all the **Clients** who commissioned this work.

Through the cooperative efforts of **Engineers and Consultants** in particular:

STRUCTURAL DESIGN
Burggraf, Weichinger & Partner GmbH
Martin & Associates Group, Inc.
Ove Arup & Partners
Schlaich, Bergermann & Partner
Sobek und Rieger
Thornton Tomasetti

MECHANICAL AND ELECTRICAL DESIGN
Cosentini Associates
Ebener & Partner
Flack + Kurtz Consulting Engineers
IC Consult
Jaros Baum & Bolles
Ove Arup & Partners

LIGHTING DESIGN
Francis Krahe & Associates
L'Observatoire International Inc.
Sylvan R Shemitz & Associates

LANDSCAPING DESIGN
Peter Walker, William Johnson & Partners

Special thanks to **Keith H. Palmer** for coordinating the preparation of this book.

We would like to thank **The Images Publishing Group, Paul Latham and Alessina Brooks,** for their invitation to participate in this monograph series.

Photography Credits:
Wayne Cable: 162 (2,3)
Glenn Cormier: 209 (3)
S. Couturier, Archipress: 203 (10)
Hans Ege: 182 (26); 187 (47, 49)
H.G. Esch: 79 (17)
Engelhardt/Sellin, Aschau I. CH., Germany: 15 (3–5); 16 (9, 10); 19 (15–19); 136 (2); 137 (3–5); 138 (7, 8); 139 (9); 140 (13); 141 (14–16); 175 (3–5); 176 (6–11); 177 (13, 14); 178 (16); 179 (17–20, 25); 201 (3, 4); 202 (5, 6); 203 (9)
Scott Francis, Esto: 90 (3); 93 (2–5); 94 (1); 115 (3, 4)
Peter Mass, Esto: 114 (1)
Courtesy of Josef Gartner & Co.: 73 (3); 74 (6)
Roland Halbe: 73 (3); 74 (4–6); 75 (7, 8); 76 (10); 77 (12); 78 (13–15); 79 (16–21)
Hedrich-Blessing: 103 (4, 5)
Timothy Hursley, The Arkansas Office: 97 (2); 98 (3); 99 (5); 109 (3–5); 110 (7–9); 111 (10); 214 (2); 215 (5); 216 (7); 217 (8, 10–11); 218 (12, 13, 15); 219 (16)
The Images Publishing Group, Tim Griffith: 17 (11); 19 (20); 203 (11)
Tim Griffith: 57 (2); 58 (3); 59 (4, 5); 60 (7, 8); 61 (9, 11); 62 (13, 14); 64 (17); 65 (19)
Helmut Jahn: Front cover; 40 (2); 41 (3); 132 (1); 133 (4, 5); 134 (6–9); 135 (10); 153 (3, 4); 181 (25); 182 (27–29); 183 (30–33); 184 (34–38); 188 (51, 52); 189 (53, 54)
Paul Kivett: 44 (2); 45 (4–6)
George Lambros: 103 (2, 3)
Nathaniel Lieberman: 115 (5)
John Linden: 15 (6, 7); 18 (13, 14); 180 (22)
John McGrail: 104 (2, 4)
Michael Meyersfeld: 122 (2); 123 (3–5)
Gregory Murphey: 166 (6)
Keith H. Palmer: 36 (3); 37 (4–5, 7–8); 38 (2); 39 (3–5); 43 (2); 48 (3); 54 (3, 4); 143 (1); 148 (2, 3); 199 (7, 8); 192 (2); 193 (3); 194 (7)
Keith H. Palmer/James Steinkamp: 23 (2); 25 (3–5); 26 (6–8); 27 (9–11); 28 (2); 29 (3–6); 30 (2, 3); 31 (4, 5); 33 (3–7); 34 (2); 35 (5); 124 (2); 125 (3); 127 (3–7); 128 (2); 129 (3); 164 (2); 165 (3); 166 (4, 5); 220 (2); 221 (3–5); 222 (1, 3)
Ryan Roulette: 208 (1); 209 (4)
Raimund Schoeck: 79 (16, 20)
Sedlacyek, courtesy of Josef Gartner & Co.: 79 (19)
Mark Segal: 167 (7)
Skyline Studio: 113 (4, 5)
Courtesy of Stahl: 79 (19)
James Steinkamp, Steinkamp/Ballogg Photography: 20 (3); 21 (4); 22 (3); 49 (2, 3); 51 (3–5); 66 (1); 67 (1); 69 (3); 81 (3, 4); 82 (2); 83 (1); 87 (3, 4); 89 (3, 5); 95 (1, 2); 100 (2, 3); 101 (2, 3); 110 (6); 159 (2, 4); 160 (2); 196 (2); 197 (3, 4); 207 (9); 211 (3, 4); 212 (5, 6); 213 (8, 9); 217 (9); 218 (13); 222 (2, 4)
Tod Swlechichowski: 75 (8)
Addison Thompson: 84 (2); 85 (3)
Lawrence S. Williams, Inc.: 105 (3); 107 (6–8)
Jay Wolke: 71 (8)
Fernado Urquijo: 203 (7); 204 (8)

Rendering Credits:
Michael Budilovsky: 50 (2); 21 (5–8); 22 (1, 2); 23 (1); 118 (2); 119 (1); 142 (1, 2); 143 (2); 151 (5); 206 (7); 198 (5, 6)
Martin Wolf: 190 (2); 191 (3–5); 193 (4); 194 (5, 6)

Index

Bold page numbers refer to projects included in Selected and Current Works.

1000 West Sixth Street, Los Angeles, California 237

11 Diagonal Street, Johannesburg, South Africa **122**, 233

1111 Brickell Avenue, Miami, Florida **100**, 237

120 North LaSalle, Chicago, Illinois **68**, 237

21 Century Tower, Shanghai, China **50**, 241

300 East 85th Street, New York, New York 235

362 West Street, Durban, South Africa **112**, 234

425 Lexington Avenue, New York, New York **90**, 235

701 Fourth Avenue South, Minneapolis, Minnesota 233

750 Lexington Avenue, New York, New York **92**, 235

9th and Figueroa, Los Angeles, California 236

Abu Dhabi Conference Center City, Abu Dhabi, United Arab Emirates **42**, 230

Alexanderplatz, Berlin, Germany 241

Alliance Airport Terminal— Administration Building, Fort Worth, Texas 246

ANL/DOE Program Support Facility, Argonne, Illinois **28**, 230

Area 2 Police Headquarters, Chicago, Illinois **30**, 230

Augustinerhof-Nuernberg, Nuernberg, Germany **158**, 244

Auraria Library, Denver, Colorado **40**, 228

Bangkok International Airport, Bangkok, Thailand **192**, 248

Bank of Southwest Tower, Houston, Texas **120**, 236

Barnett Center, Jacksonville, Florida **84**, 237

Caltex House, Singapore **56**, 238

Canadian Broadcast Tower, Toronto, Canada 239

Celebration Center, Orlando, Florida **20**, 232

Charlemagne, Brussels, Belgium **142**, 245

Chicago Board Of Trade Addition, Chicago, Illinois **124**, 233

Citizens & Southern Bank, Atlanta, Georgia 239

Cityspire, New York, New York **94**, 235

COD/Learning Resources Center, Glen Ellyn, Illinois 231

Codex Corporate Headquarters, Canton, Massachusetts 231

Columbus Circle, New York, New York **119**, 236

Columbus Pier, Hamburg, Germany 245

Commonwealth Edison District Headquarters, Bolingbrook, Illinois 229

Communication Center FFM, Frankfurt, Germany 244

Credit Lyonnais Bank Nederland, Rotterdam, The Netherlands 238

De La Garza Career Center, East Chicago, Indiana **32**, 229

Dearborn Station, Dearborn, Michigan **180**, 248

Dockland Square, London, England 239

Endless Towers **54**, 241

Europa-Haus, Frankfurt, Germany **160**, 244

Exposition and Office Complex, Chicago, Illinois 231

FAA O'Hare Control Tower, Chicago, Illinois **82**, 240

First & Broadway Los Angeles Civic Center, Los Angeles, California **163**, 242

First Source Center, South Bend, Indiana **170**, 242

Flughafen Koln/Bonn Terminal One, Cologne, Germany **196**, 248

Fort Canning Tower, Singapore **66**, 240

Fountain Square West, Cincinnati, Ohio **80**, 240

Fourth District Courts Building, Maywood, Illinois 228

H. Roe Bartle Exhibition Hall, Kansas City, Missouri 228

Hague Town Hall and Library, Amsterdam, The Netherlands 242

Harold Washington Library Center Competition, Chicago, Illinois **162**, 243

Hitachi Tower, Singapore **56**, 238

Hotel Kempinski/Munich Airport Center/ Walkways, Munich, Germany **174**, 247

Hyatt Regency Roissy, Roissy, Charles De Gaule, France **200**, 247

IHZ Tower, Düsseldorf, Germany **67**, 240

Jakarta Communications Tower **48**, 241

Jakarta Tower Kuningan Centre, Jakarta, Indonesia **49**, 241

JFK Consolidated Terminal, Jamaica, New York **210**, 247

John Marshall Courts Building, Richmond, Virginia 228

Kemper Arena Kansas City, Missouri **44**, 228

King Abdulaziz International Airport Competition, Jeddah, Saudi Arabia **204**, 248

Ku-Damm 119, Berlin, Germany **152**, 243

Ku-Damm 70, Berlin, Germany **132**, 243

Kuala Lumpur City Center 1, Kuala Lumpur, Malaysia **83**, 240

La Lumiere Gymnasium, La Porte, Indiana 230

Landesgirokasse Bank Center, Stuttgart, Germany 244

Livingston Plaza, Brooklyn Heights, New York 242

Lufthansa Corporate Headquarters, Köln, Germany **161**, 244

Mannheimer Lebensversicherung Headquarters, Mannheim, Germany **154**, 243

Merchandise Mart Bridge, Chicago, Illinois 246

Messe Hall 1, Frankfurt, Germany 232

Messe Riem Urban Competition, Munich, Germany 232

Messe Tower/Messe Hall, Frankfurt, Germany **72**, 235

Metro West, Naperville, Illinois **116**, 234

Michigan City Public Library, Michigan City, Indiana **38**, 229

Minnesota Government & History Center, St Paul, Minnesota **43**, 229

Monarch Beach Office Building, Dana Point, California 232

Munich Order Center, Munich, Germany **14**, 232

Navy Pier, Chicago, Illinois **22**, 232

The North Loop Block 37, Chicago, Illinois **101**, 238

Northwestern Atrium Center, Chicago, Illinois **108**, 234

O'Hare Rapid Transit Station, Chicago, Illinois **220**, 246

Oakbrook Post Office, Oakbrook, Illinois 230

Oakbrook Terrace Tower, Oakbrook Terrace, Illinois **102**, 235

One America Plaza 237

One America Plaza/Trolley Station, San Diego, California **208**, 247

One Liberty Place, Philadelphia, Pennsylvania **104**, 234

One South Wacker, Chicago, Illinois **126**, 233

Pacific Basin Tower 236

Palace Prince Khaled, Saudi Arabia 232

Pallas Office Building, Stuttgart, Germany **136**, 243

Park Avenue Tower, New York, New York **114**, 234

Parktown Stands, Johannesburg, South Africa 231

Plaza East, Milwaukee, Wisconsin 233

Principal Mutual Life Insurance Company, Des Moines, Iowa **143**, 245

Project J (1, 2, 3), Chicago, Illinois **95**, 238

Reichstagsgebaude Competition, Berlin, Germany 245

Rust-Oleum Corporation Headquarters, Vernon Hills, Illinois **34**, 229

San Diego Convention Center, San Diego, California **23**, 231

Shand Morahan Corporate Headquarters, Evanston, Illinois **168**, 242

Sony Center Berlin, Berlin, Germany **148**, 245

South Ferry Plaza, New York, New York **118**, 236

St Mary's Athletic Facility, South Bend, Indiana **36**, 229

State Of Illinois Center, Chicago, Illinois **164**, 242

Stralauer Platz 35, Berlin, Germany **144**, 245

Stuttgart/Berliner Platz, Stuttgart, Germany 237

Television City, New York, New York 236

Tokyo Teleport Town, Tokyo, Japan **88**, 239

Tokyu-Shibuya Tower, Tokyo, Japan **55**, 241

Two Liberty Place, Philadelphia, Pennsylvania 237

United Airlines Terminal One Complex, O'Hare Airport, Chicago, Illinois **214**, 246

University of Illinois Agricultural Engineering Science Building, Champaign, Illinois 230

Victoria Düsseldorf Competition, Düsseldorf, Germany 242

Victoria/Victoria City Areal, Berlin, Germany 244

Victoria Versicherungsgesellshaft **150**, 244

Wan-Chai Competition, Hong Kong 239

West Loop Pedway, Chicago, Illinois 246

Wilshire/Westwood, Los Angeles, California **96**, 234

Wisconsin Residence, Eagle River, Wisconsin **24**, 231

World's Tallest Building 239

Xerox Centre, Chicago, Illinois **128**, 233

Yokohama Waterfront MM21 Project, Yokohama, Japan **86**, 240

Every effort has been made to trace the original source of copyright material contained in this book. The publishers would be pleased to hear from copyright holders to rectify any errors or omissions.

The information and illustrations in this publication have been prepared and supplied by Murphy/Jahn. While all reasonable efforts have been made to ensure accuracy, the publishers do not, under any circumstances, accept responsibility for errors, omissions and representations express or implied.